The Politics of British Feminism, 1918–1970

The Politics of British Feminism, 1918–1970

Olive Banks

Edward Elgar

Published by
Edward Elgar Publishing Limited
Gower House
Croft Road
Aldershot
Hants GU11 3HR
England

Edward Elgar Publishing Company
Old Post Road
Brookfield
Vermont 05036
USA

British Library Cataloguing in Publication Data
Banks, Olive
  Politics of British Feminism, 1918–70
  I. Title
  305.420941

Library of Congress Cataloguing in Publication Data
Banks, Olive
    The politics of British feminism, 1918–70 / Olive Banks.
    160 p. 21 cm.
    Includes bibliographical references and index.
    1. Feminism—Great Britain—History—20th century.   2. Women—
Great Britain—Social conditions.   I. Title.
JQ1593.B33   1993
305.42'0941—dc20   93–18896
                                                                                CIP

ISBN 1 85278 108 4
     1 85278 900 X (Paperback)

Printed in Great Britain at the University Press, Cambridge

Contents

1. Introduction

The Act of 1918, giving the majority of women the right to the Parliamentary suffrage, began a new era for the women's movement in which it had to face quite different challenges. The struggle for the vote had dominated the movement from the 1860s onwards, reaching a climax in the decade immediately preceding the first world war, so that, by 1918, the vote had become not only a symbol of women's entry into the rights of citizenship, but the key to unlock all the other doors still closed to them. True the Act of 1918 was a rather uneasy compromise which left many women still unenfranchised but it was recognized that the principle had been won and it was expected that the full enfranchisement of women would not be long delayed. By 1928, indeed, the process of enfranchisement was complete. Furthermore, a second Act of 1918 had given women over 21 the right to sit in the House of Commons.

For some women who had been active in the suffrage movement, the struggle if not by 1918 then certainly by 1928 seemed virtually over and of these women many moved gratefully to other causes or even away from politics altogether (Banks, 1986). With hindsight we now know how mistaken that view was and the enfranchisement of women has sometimes seemed to modern feminists a very empty victory. Certainly, even on the most optimistic assessment enfranchisement has achieved much less for women than was hoped for by those who worked so devotedly for the cause for so many years. In the chapters that follow an attempt will be made to add to our understanding of this particular period in the history of feminism, between the achievement of citizenship in 1918 and the rise of the modern women's movement at the end of the 1960s.

This particular period, although, in my view, one of tremendous significance, has not attracted the same attention from historians as the more dramatic suffrage struggle which immediately preceded it. None of the campaigns between 1918 and 1970 had the same epic quality, and there were none of the episodes of violence and even martyrdom.

Nor were there any charismatic heroines to compare with the women of the Pankhurst family. It is possible, too, that the very nature of feminism during this period has deterred researchers. During the inter-war period it became so splintered into different organizations and different factions that it has been impossible to avoid asking whether it can be described as a movement at all. Moreover the unity between feminism and socialism which distinguished much of the suffrage campaign was gradually weakened in the years after the first world war.

Nevertheless there has been a growing interest both in the interwar years and in the postwar period, as well as in the war years themselves, and this has provided not only new information but in some cases a useful new approach. There are still gaps in our knowledge, especially of several important feminist groups, and a number of important cam-paigns have not been given a detailed and comprehensive study. There is still for example no complete account of the equal pay campaign in spite of the work of historians like Harold Smith who has contributed greatly to our understanding of the campaign during the second world war. (Smith, 1981; Smith, 1984a).

There has also, with one recent exception, been no detailed attempt at an overview of the period as a whole. Doughan has, it is true, contributed such an overview but, in what is only a brief paper, he could not do more than outline the main issues as he saw them. More-over his paper, although still useful, is now beginning to be out of date (Doughan, 1980). The same must be said of my own outline of the period (Banks, 1981). Part of a much wider study of feminist history, the period ranging from 1918 to 1980 was necessarily sketched only briefly. Moreover it, too, is out of date. The collection of papers edited by Harold Smith, although it covers the whole period from 1900 to the 1980s, takes the form of individual contributions linked only by their addition to our understanding of particular aspects of twentieth cen-tury feminism (Smith, 1990).

The studies available therefore provide us in the main with only a limited and in many respects a partial view. Those which do cover most or all of the period examine either individual campaigns in detail, or look at particular issues. There is also a number of detailed investi-gations of certain, sometimes short, periods of time. Many of these have been invaluable sources for constructing an overview of the whole period, but do not provide such an overview in themselves. The nearest approach to what I have in mind is the account by Elizabeth

Wilson of the postwar period, which she calls, imaginatively, *Only Halfway to Paradise* (Wilson, 1980). This too is now becoming out of date. Moreover by leaving out the whole period between 1918 and 1945 it does not provide the kind of overview which is the aim of the present study.

The one study which does present an overview of the period was published when this study was almost complete (Pugh, 1992). Written by the historian, Martin Pugh, it covers the women's movement between 1914 and 1959, and in doing so deals with many of the aspects which have been central to the present study. Nevertheless the overlap is by no means complete since his main emphasis is on the interwar period and there is no attempt to deal with the 1960s, which were years of very great significance for the women's movement, even before the rise of the new movement in the last years of that decade. Nor is there any systematic attempt to analyse the context in which the women's movement was forced to struggle and which is treated in considerable detail in the second half of this volume. Most significantly of all, Pugh and I approach the subject matter from very different perspectives and in some respects, though not in all, reach different conclusions, more especially on the influence of the so-called 'new' feminism but also on the role of women in Parliament. For example, I clearly place a great deal more emphasis on the part played by them in the struggle for feminism. In this context I give special attention to the conflict of loyalty between gender and party which placed great strain on many women MPs in both the major parties. Indeed, to a much greater extent than Pugh I see the constraint of party politics and especially the opposition of party leaders and governments as more important factors in the failure to make progress with issues, such as equal pay, than weaknesses in the women's movement itself.

At the same time I take a more hostile approach to 'new' feminism than Pugh does, especially during the 1950s when it helped to buttress an essentially anti-feminist ideology which deeply influenced feminism itself. Perhaps the chief difference between our interpretations, however, is that whereas Pugh sees the historical process he describes as largely one of evolution, I see it as one of conflict in which forces of conservatism, not only within the Conservative Party but in the labour and trade union movement, were concerned to maintain a traditional view of women's role and an ideology of separate spheres between men and women which feminism has tried to challenge. Nevertheless his book does provide a great deal of new and valuable information, especially on the 1920s and 1930s, which throws fresh light on many aspects of the period, some of which have not been given prominence in the present study.

As in Pugh's book, however, the women's movement has a central place, and some definition of what is meant by the term would seem to be in order here. It has been used fairly loosely to include those groups or organizations run by, and for, women with a concern for women's affairs generally and with more or less specific and deliberate attempts to make things better for women. This aim, however, has not been the sole criterion for inclusion of an organization and several groups have been included which were part of a wider movement with quite different aims. The Women's Co-operative Guild for example saw its aims as including the spread of cooperative ideals but it was also concerned with a variety of specifically women's issues which sometimes brought it into conflict with the wider movement. In order to maintain the distinction, however, the two kinds of organization have been grouped into separate chapters, one on autonomous and in the main feminist groups, and one on women's organizations within labour, cooperative and trade union movements. Although treated separately, however, the links between them will be prominent in the analysis.

Chapter 3 looks at women in Parliament. One of the important changes introduced in 1918 was the actual presence of women in the House of Commons. For a number of years they were no more than a token presence and were never more than a small minority but there is no doubt that from the very first a woman's voice in the House did make a difference. Although by no means all women MPs were feminists and indeed, as several studies have shown, women's issues occupied only a limited proportion of their time (Harrison, 1986; Brookes, 1967), they nevertheless did a great deal, as this particular chapter will show, to bring women's issues to the attention of the House of Commons. There were, of course, several problems facing those women MPs who wished to pursue women's interests in Parliament and these problems will be examined in some detail. Party loyalty was perhaps the most important since it is political parties and their interests which dominate and even control the House of Commons but the fact that women were never more than a tiny minority, unable to carry their views without considerable male support, has also reduced their impact on the decisions of the House.

If, however, a study of women's organizations on the one hand, and women MPs on the other, presents us with a general picture of the women's movement in terms of both its aims and its achievements, the attempt to explain both its successes and its failures cannot be understood without an examination of the context in which it was forced to operate. This context, therefore, will be the subject matter of Part II of the book. Neither of the major political parties, for example, in spite of occasional support, was really sympathetic to many of the claims of the women's movement and every success finally achieved was only won after what was sometimes a very long, hard struggle. Moreover there was not only a struggle against indifference but also a direct confrontation between differing ideologies concerning the role of women. It will be argued in Chapter 5, that anti-feminism was deeply rooted within the labour and trade union movement as well as in the Conservative Party. It also dominated the higher levels of the civil service, as well as the professions. Many of the intellectual movements both during the interwar period and certainly throughout the 1940s and 1950s were deeply hostile to the aspirations of feminism. Moreover even sections of the women's movement itself held deeply conservative views with respect to women.

Although the ideological context in which the women's movement operated remained relatively constant the political context was to some extent a changing one. Political leaders had to take into account pressures from within their own parties, but also from the electorate, which had the power to place them in office or to remove them from it. Consequently decisions on women's issues were made on political as well as ideological grounds. Moreover after 1918 leaders of both main parties had for the first time to take account of the wishes of an electorate which not only included women, but in which after 1928 women were in a majority. Women, too, were a force within the parties themselves, and their pressure could at times be highly significant. Political leaders could therefore accept the claims of the women's movement as a result of purely political considerations, irrespective of their ideological position; Chapter 6 will show that this happened on a number of occasions.

Another important context which must be considered is that of the economic situation which frequently influenced the attitude of the government towards women's claims. The achievement of equal pay for example was constantly hindered by economic crises of one kind or another, whereas a sharp rise in the demand for women's labour influenced government policy to women's advantage with respect to both equal pay and the marriage bar. Some of the ways in which the

state of the economy both helped and hindered the women's movement will be examined in Chapter 8.

The aim of the study as a whole is very simple. It seeks both to
describe and to understand what happened to the women's movement
and necessarily also to feminism after the victory of the suffrage
campaign and before the arrival of the modern women's movement in
the late 1960s. Although it did not disappear altogether, and indeed in
every decade from the 1920s onwards there is evidence of its activity,
there is no doubt that for the whole period of this study it seemed to be
a movement in decline. The war years saw a resurgence of feminist
campaigning but during the 1950s it seemed to be submerged under a
mystique of femininity which came to dominate even feminism itself
(Wilson, 1980). There were still individual feminists, it is true, and I
was one myself, but even feminists came to doubt, as I did, whether
there was any longer a feminist movement (Banks and Banks, 1964).
The rise of a lively new feminism in the late 1960s revealed these fears
to have been unfounded, for in spite of the decline of the movement it
was obvious that feminism was far from dead.

Yet, in the light of that resurgence the need to understand what
happened to both the women's movement and to feminism becomes
more urgent, not less. It is hoped that the present study will do something to add to that understanding, although I would not want to claim
too much. There are still serious gaps in our knowledge of the period,
especially as regards the women's movement; in addition the issues
involved are of necessity extremely complex. Nevertheless the very
neglect of the period in the past has meant that the task of appraisal
and reassessment has become more, not less, urgent. The book therefore should be read as part of the ongoing process of recreating feminist history.

The emphasis of the book is on the organized women's movement
as it existed from 1918, when women were first admitted to the parliamentary franchise, and the late 1960s when the modern women's movement may be said to have begun. It is generally agreed that this was a
movement which had its roots outside the existing women's organizations, some of which were indeed unsympathetic towards its. It represented something quite new, and, although there were significant ideological links, they were not necessarily recognized at the time and
many leading feminists who emerged in the late 1960s and 1970s had
very little knowledge of what has since come to be described as 'first
wave' feminism. I have, consequently, not tried to explore the roots of

the new women's movement even though they were emerging during the 1960s, believing that they form part of a separate although equally important study. I have been concerned to describe only the impact of the new movement on existing organizations and, in Chapter 4, on women MPs.

It is also necessary to emphasize that, as the title indicates, this is a book primarily about politics. Two major chapters are based largely on Parliamentary records and are concerned with political parties and especially with the role of governments in the success or failure of women's campaigns. The two chapters specifically on the women's movement also have a strongly political slant, dealing as they do with the attempt by various women's organizations to influence a political party or the government itself. This reflects my own view of the significance of the political perspective although of course other viewpoints could be brought to bear on either feminism or the women's movement. Indeed, some sections of the women's liberation movement have rejected the political approach altogether. This was not however true of the period from 1918 to 1970, and it seemed to me to be important to analyse the success and failure of feminism at that time in terms of this particular perspective.

Finally, I would not wish to claim too much. There is still a great deal to learn about the period under review and many questions to answer. This is particularly true of the 1960s, which were crucial years in the history of feminism but about which little is known. Nevertheless, it is hoped that a survey of this kind which attempts to take a longer view of the whole period than has previously been attempted, will contribute both new answers and, perhaps even more significantly, new questions to add to our knowledge of the history of feminism.

PART I
The Progress of Feminism after Suffrage

2. The Feminists

This chapter is concerned with those women's organizations which were run by women in the interests of women, and whose aims and objectives can, in varying degrees, be described as feminist. Although by no means all the same, and indeed sometimes in conflict with each other, they shared many of the same perspectives and, as this chapter will show, held many goals in common. Many, although not all, were former suffrage organizations and a number of their leading members had served in the suffrage cause, so that it may be argued that they were part of an older feminist tradition.

In 1918 the main suffrage organization still in existence was the National Union of Women's Suffrage Societies (NUWSS), the constitutional wing of the prewar suffrage movement. Its rival, the Women's Social and Political Union (WSPU), led by Emmeline Pankhurst and her daughter, Christabel, had been disbanded at the outbreak of war in a wave of patriotic fervour on the part of the two Pankhursts. This left the NUWSS to take the lead in the negotiations during the war which led to the 1918 Act and gave the organization a special importance in the years after the war.

Apart from the NUWSS the most important suffrage group to survive the war was the Women's Freedom League. This was itself a breakaway from the WSPU and represented a similar, if less violent, militant tradition. Never a large organization even in its heyday, it continued to represent a more radical tradition in feminism. It was however dependent on the energy and financial generosity of a handful of leaders (Smith, 1990; Pugh, 1992). The International Woman Suffrage Alliance also survived the war although, as its name implies, it was always international rather than national in the range of its activities and interests. Concerned at the time of its foundation in Washington largely with the international enfranchisement of women, in 1920 it expanded its activities to include sex equality in practically all spheres of life (Whittick, 1979).

A second international organization, the International Council of Women, founded as early as 1888, was conceived largely as an umbrella organization of other women's groups. It did not at its inception concern itself with suffrage, but was involved nevertheless in a wide range of other women's issues. In Britain it was known as the National Union of Women Workers, and was a largely middle-class organization of women involved in various forms of voluntary work. Later it became the British Council of Women and as such played an important role as a women's pressure group. A conservative rather than a radical organization, it nevertheless worked with other women's groups in a variety of feminist causes (International Council of Women, 1966; Harrison, 1987).

The war years also saw the emergence of a new organization from within the NUWSS itself. In 1915 there was a serious dispute within the leadership on the issue of pacifism, a dispute which eventually split the organization virtually in half. A new organization was formed, the Women's International League for Peace and Freedom which attracted many members of the NUWSS who could not accept its stand on the war, and who after the war was over, preferred to work for an international organization (Liddington, 1989; Bussey and Timms, 1980).

During the 1920s the NUWSS, now the National Union of Societies for Equal Citizenship (NUSEC), was certainly the most important of the women's groups, working for equal rights. The change of name marked a broadening of its objectives, which took it well beyond suffrage, and the change of leadership from Millicent Fawcett to Eleanor Rathbone was, later, to produce a radical change of policy. Under her leadership and with the able assistance of Eva Hubback as secretary, NUSEC played a central and indeed crucial role in the feminist lobby, sponsoring much of the Parliamentary legislation on women's issues which marked the 1920s. In the process it forged close links with several women MPs, and especially with Nancy Astor, links which will be examined in more detail in a later chapter (Alberti, 1989).

The early 1920s also saw the formation of the Six Point Group. Founded in 1920 by Lady Rhondda, it was rather more militant than NUSEC and saw itself indeed as a descendant of the WSPU rather than the NUWSS. Too little is known about its history but it seems to have attracted women who were more radical in their approach to feminism than the women in NUSEC. It also, perhaps because of its links with Lady Rhondda's journal, *Time and Tide*, was more attractive to feminist intellectuals. Winifred Holtby and Vera Brittain were both members and so was the veteran feminist, Elizabeth Robins (Spender, 1984; Alberti, 1989).

An examination of women's groups associated directly with the labour and trade union movement has been reserved for another chapter, but the National Union of Women Teachers (NUWT) presents us with a special case. Although a trade union, the NUWT was heavily involved in a wide range of feminist issues outside its members' professional concern as teachers. The struggle for equal pay was, it is true, their central concern, as was the fight against the marriage bar, but they were also active for many years in a number of other campaigns. At the same time their links were with other feminist groups rather than with the labour and trade union movement (Pierotti, 1963).

The groups described so far were all concerned with the issue of women's rights or women's emancipation in a very general sense but, during the 1920s in particular, there was a number of more specialist groups working for a specific goal. The London and National Society for Women's Services, for example, was concerned with expanding women's professional employment and was heavily involved in the campaign to open the higher civil service to women (Harrison, 1987). Another group, the League of the Church Militant, formerly the Church League for Women's Suffrage, worked for sex equality in the Church of England. A vigorous body, although it could claim few successes, it worked principally for the ordination of women (Heeney, 1988). Yet another campaigning body was the Association for Moral and Social Hygiene. Originating during the campaign against the Contagious Diseases Acts in the 1870s, its main work was opposition to the state regulation of prostitution, but its activities widened during the twentieth century to include the fight for equal laws with respect to soliciting. Under its active secretary, Alison Nielans, its campaign to raise the age of consent to 16 had a successful outcome in the Criminal Law Amendment Act of 1922 (Jeffreys, 1985, Alberti, 1989).

Apart from the activities of a variety of women's groups working independently the 1920s also provided numerous examples of collaboration between them. For example, in 1921 Nancy Astor set up a Consultative Committee on Women's Organizations to coordinate women's political work (Harrison, 1987). Similarly, Lady Rhondda formed an Equal Political Rights Committee. There were also numerous examples of groups working closely together in support of particular issues (Alberti, 1989). The first major campaign of the Six Point Group, for example, concerned the Criminal Law Amendment Bill of 1921 and in doing so worked closely with the Association for Moral Hygiene. The Council of Women was also prominent in this campaign.

The issue of women in the police force was also one which involved several different organizations. During the first world war the National Council of Women had organized women police patrols, largely because of their concern for the traffic in young girls, and after the war the issue was taken up by both NUSEC and the Six Point Group (Carrier, 1988). Moreover both NUSEC and the National Council of Women were associated with the League of the Church Militant in their campaign for the ordination of women (Heeney, 1988). The suffrage campaign during the 1920s to extend the right to vote to all women also brought together all the feminist groups in joint activities and there was pressure too from the international organizations, the Women's International League and the International Woman Suffrage Alliance which itself maintained close links with NUSEC during the 1920s (Alberti, 1989). Other issues which brought the feminist groups together included equal guardianship of children, the right of peeresses to sit in the House of Lords, the right of married women to work, and the right of women to retain their citizenship on marriage.

The major impression therefore is of a considerable degree of co-operation. Each of these groups retained its independence and even its individuality but they were prepared to work together to achieve common goals. There were, however, important areas of disagreement and in time these served to create dissension of a damaging kind. These disagreements centred around Eleanor Rathbone's vigorous advocacy of what became known as 'new' feminism, and more especially her claim that the old equal rights feminism was out of date, which led to a deepening of controversy. It was Rathbone's contention that the majority of women were destined to be mothers, and it was their needs as mothers with which NUSEC should be concerned. Consequently she argued that the preoccupation with equal rights, which had for so long been feminism's concern, was no longer appropriate now that so many basic rights had been achieved. In particular she believed that the claim for equal pay should wait until an adequate system of family endowment had been achieved (Land, 1990).

While Rathbone's arguments appealed to many within NUSEC they alarmed and antagonized others and created a serious division between NUSEC and the Six Point Group. Her critics within both organizations did not necessarily disagree with her championing of family endowment or her support for birth control, but they did disagree with her claim that the equal rights battle was virtually won. Both Vera Brittain and Winifred Holtby, for example, were active members of the Six Point Group who approved of both family allowances and birth control but who called themselves 'old' rather than 'new' feminists because they believed that equal rights were far from achieved (Berry and Bishop, 1985; Gorham, 1990). They also disliked the emphasis on motherhood which characterized the 'new' feminism. While they wanted a proper respect for maternity, they resented any undue emphasis upon it which they saw as circumscribing the activities of women in an unnecessary way (Kent, 1990; Holtby, 1934). In particular both Brittain and Holtby were vehemently opposed to any solution to the problems of maternity which deprived women of their right to work. Whereas the 'new' feminists saw most women as necessarily confined to the home, 'old' feminists like Brittain and Holtby looked to new and more elastic forms of domestic organization in order to release women from their thraldom to the household.

On the whole the Six Point Group were not to accept Rathbone's ideas but NUSEC was more sympathetic and in 1926 both family endowment and birth control became NUSEC policy. What finally split the organization was a proposed change in the attitude to protective legislation (Pugh, 1992). Initially NUSEC, like other feminist groups, was opposed to any legislation which limited women's employment opportunities (Smith, 1990), but by the mid-1920s there were growing pressures from within the organization for a change of policy. Undoubtedly the main source of these pressures was those members who were sympathetic to the support for protective legislation, found within the labour and trade union movement, and who believed sincerely that such legislation was necessary if working women were to be protected from harmful working conditions and excessive hours of work. By 1926 sympathy for this point of view was sufficient to produce a majority vote in support of protective legislation at the annual conference. It succeeded however only by a small margin, and opposition within NUSEC led eleven members of the executive to resign (Kent, 1988; Alberti, 1989).

Other feminist organizations remained opposed to protective legislation, including the Six Point Group. Both Holtby and Brittain, in spite of their sympathies with the labour movement, had serious doubts about its consequences, since they believed that it carried the implication that women were the weaker sex. Brittain also argued against special privileges for women, since she believed that they weakened women's claim for equal status and equal pay (Holtby, 1934; Brittain, 1928). Another feminist opposed to protective legislation was the American-born Crystal Eastman. Although a socialist who supported both birth control and family endowment, she rejected protective legislation as ultimately harmful to women's interests (Cook, 1978). As a result of the controversy a new organization, the Open Door Council, was formed in 1926, specifically to oppose restrictions on women's employment opportunities, followed in 1929 by an international organization to work at the international level (Smith, 1990; Alberti, 1989).

The division within NUSEC not only harmed the organization itself by depriving it of some of its most active leaders; it also sharpened the differences between NUSEC and other feminist groups. The National Union of Women Teachers, for example, which was affiliated to NUSEC, turned instead to the Six Point Group and the Open Door Council. The NUWT not only opposed protective legislation for women but were angered by Eleanor Rathbone's attempts to link family allowances and equal pay. Although not opposed to the principle of family allowances, they believed that the case for equal pay was a matter of justice to women and had nothing to do with family commitments (Pierotti, 1963). By 1928, indeed, differences between the member groups forced the closure of the Consultative Committee of Women's Organizations, founded by Nancy Astor in 1921 (Harrison, 1987; Alberti, 1989; Smith, 1990). In spite of these differences there was still sufficient common ground to ensure collaboration between the various groups on such issues as the extension of the franchise, finally achieved in 1928. Moreover when in 1929 a Women Peers Committee was set up to work for the admission of peeresses to the House of Lords, it included representatives from NUSEC as well as the WFL (Women's Freedom League) and the NUWT.

By 1929, however, the days of NUSEC's pre-eminence were over, and in the next few years it declined rapidly, both in the size of its membership and in its influence. Part of the reason for this decline was the split in the executive on the issue of protective legislation. This deprived it of many of its leading equal rights feminists and strengthened the supporters of the 'new' feminists who believed that the majority of equal rights had already been achieved. The later 1920s saw a move away from the political lobbying which dominated the first half of the decade, and a new programme was developed with a predominantly educational aim. To further this programme a completely new organization was formed, the Townswomen's Guild.

Founded in 1928 it was largely modelled on the Women's Institutes and was intended to attract women who were not in any sense feminist. Indeed any feminist programme was deliberately avoided in order to keep the Guild open to all women, whatever their personal views, as well as to attract grants.

Throughout most of its history the Townswomen's Guild has remained aloof from other women's groups and it was not until the late 1950s that there was a move towards a political role, when the Guild joined in the widespread lobbying on the part of women's groups against the use of turnstiles in public lavatories. Moreover, although it has always emphasized its mainly educational role, its chief interest has always been in arts and crafts. This was not necessarily in the minds of its founders, who were more interested in education for citizenship, but it was clearly a response to the interests of its members which were focused on the traditional skills of the housewife (Stott, 1978). In 1928 there does not seem to have been any intention of abandoning NUSEC itself, and it was envisaged that existing NUSEC branches would continue as before. It was soon obvious however that this was not to be. The number of branches shrank rapidly and in 1933 its journal, *The Woman Leader*, ceased publication. By the end of the war only the Townswomen's Guild remained (Harrison, 1987; Pugh, 1992).

It is not clear how far the decline in NUSEC can be directly attributed to the foundation of the Guild. Certainly some of the NUSEC leadership devoted their time and attention to the Guild rather than to NUSEC itself and this could not have been unimportant. The change of attitude to protective legislation and the advocacy of the so-called 'new' feminism certainly alienated those who saw themselves as old or equal rights feminists. There may also have been a loss of interest in specifically feminist concerns as, during the 1930s in particular, the issue of large-scale unemployment and the threat of war appeared to many women to be of more pressing concern

The issues of peace and collective security had been significant within the women's movement since the first world war, and, indeed a number of former suffrage workers had chosen to work at the international rather than the national level as soon as the war was over (Alberti, 1989). By the 1930s issues of war and peace took on an increasing importance and even as active an equal rights feminist as Vera Brittain was, by the mid-1930s, writing mainly on pacifist rather than feminist themes (Berry and Bishop, 1985). The peace movement itself was neither a feminist nor indeed a women's movement (Liddington, 1989), but many women did see peace as a feminist issue and identified militarism in particular with masculine values. Although these ideas were prevalent in the first world war, the most striking and perhaps best known exposition of the links between masculinity and militarism is Virginia Woolf's *Three Guineas*, published just before the outbreak of the second world war. In this powerful and outspoken treatise she argued that men and women see the world through different eyes, and that a love of fighting is a male, not a female attribute.

If, however, pacifism and feminism were closely linked by women like Virginia Woolf and Vera Brittain, there is no doubt that the links depended on a move away from equal rights feminism, and towards the 'new' feminism with its emphasis on the differences between men and women rather than their similarities. The development of Vera Brittain's pacifism, for example, brought a change in her feminism. She came to believe not only that men and women had different needs and abilities but that war actually violated women's biology (Mellown, 1985). The peace movement itself had a wide appeal to women's organizations, however, even to those committed to equal rights rather than to 'new' feminism. The Women's Peace Crusade, a great pilgrimage of women held in 1926, involved as many as 28 women's organizations. This included a wide variety of groups, ranging from the conservative National Council of Women to the radical National Union of Women Teachers (Pierotti, 1963).

The unemployment of the 1930s and especially the poverty associated with it had a profound effect on the women's movement. There was particular anxiety at the effect of poverty on children and during the 1930s the Children's Minimum Council was the main pressure group, arguing for measures to reduce the effect of child poverty. Growing information on the extent of poverty, especially in large families, also fuelled support for family allowances. Indeed, in spite of a great deal of suspicion from the labour and trade union movement there was a great deal of support from women's organizations both within the labour movement and outside. The birth control movement also attracted wide support from women's groups. NUSEC for example came out in favour in 1926 and the National Council of Women in 1929 (Leathard, 1980). By the 1930s too there was growing interest amongst women's groups on the subject of abortion, sparked off by the large numbers of deaths in childbirth, believed to be to some extent the effect of illegal abortions. The National Council of Women was particularly anxious about the figures on maternal mortality and harassed the Ministry of Health on the issue. In October 1935, not long before the foundation of the Abortion Law Reform Association in 1936, they advocated a committee of enquiry and in 1935 passed the first of a series of resolutions, calling for abortion law reform (Hindell and Simms, 1971). Like family allowances these two issues, birth control and abortion, brought together women from feminist organizations and, as we shall see in the next chapter, women from the labour movement. This was because both the birth control movement and the abortion law reform campaign were able to take advantage of current anxieties about maternal mortality and morbidity and the health of working-class mothers in general.

If, however, the 'new' feminism appeared to be gaining ground in the 1930s this is not to suggest that equal rights feminism had disappeared. The Six Point Group continued to exist, mainly as a London-based pressure group (Pugh, 1992), as well as more specialist groups, like the London Society for Women's Service. This became independent of NUSEC in 1929 and, under the leadership of Ray Strachey, concerned itself largely with career opportunities. The NUWT continued to be highly active, working not only for the rights of women teachers but for a very wide range of other feminist issues. There was also a number of coordinating committees formed for specific purposes. The Woman Peers Committee had been set up in 1929 and its efforts continued throughout the 1930s. There was also an active Nationality of Married Women Committee which sought to secure to women the right to retain their British nationality on marriage.

The divisions within feminism, therefore, weakened it but did not destroy it, although it tended to be fragmented into a series of single-issue campaigns. There was no great cause comparable to the fight for the vote which had had the power to unite all the women's groups into a single movement. Organizations differed not only in terms of their priorities but even more fundamentally in terms of their definition of feminism itself.

The immediate effect of the second world war was to give a fresh boost to equal rights feminism and particularly the equal pay campaign. The argument for equal pay for equal work had long been a feminist objective and one which was able to unite both the equal rights feminists and the women's trade union movement. In 1934, for example, as many as 33 women's organizations combined in an equal pay campaign (Pierotti, 1963). Successive governments had however been adamant in their rejection of such claims and, in spite of the need for women's labour in war work and in the services, the wartime coalition government refused to make concessions, even in the case of women who had been conscripted despite the protests from a number of women's organizations, spearheaded by the Six Point Group (Smith, 1981). The only exception was in the case of a small number of women in engineering who were doing men's work, and this particular concession was made in response to demands not from women's organizations but from trade unionists, anxious to protect the male rate of pay.

Nevertheless, the campaign in support of equal pay continued throughout the war and, in the case of compensation for war injuries, achieved its only success. Under the Personal Injuries (Emergency Provisions) Act of 1939 compensation for men and women civilians was not only set at different rates, but differed as between single men and single women, since married men were able to claim a dependents' allowance. These provisions led to an outcry that resulted in a major campaign in which women's organizations and women members of Parliament combined and succeeded in defeating the government. As early as January 1941, members of over 40 women's organizations sent a deputation to the Minister of Pensions, and in the following October a pressure group was established, the Equal Compensation Campaign, with representatives from a wide range of organizations. Eventually, as a result of pressure within Parliament itself which will be described in a later chapter, a select committee was appointed and in 1943 the government agreed to provide equal compensation for single men and single women, with extra payment for both the wives and the children of those men who were married (Smith, 1981).

Nevertheless, although the campaign was rightly regarded as a notable victory, it had little effect on the equal pay issue in general. Yet support for equal pay continued to grow, especially after the success of the equal compensation campaign and in 1944 an Equal Pay Campaign Committee was established with the immediate objective of equal pay in the civil service. It included representatives from the Six Point Group, the Fawcett Society, and the Open Door Council, and continued to be active until equal pay in the public services was achieved in 1956 (Potter, 1957).

The war years also saw an attempt to introduce an anti-discrimination bill which would have established equal rights for women by law. Mainly the work of Dorothy Evans of the Six Point Group, it obtained the support of a number of feminists, including Vera Brittain and Edith Summerskill, but none of the political parties was prepared to endorse it. The death of Dorothy Evans in August 1944 effectively ended the campaign (Doughan, 1980). Another feminist organization active during the war was the Women's Freedom League. Although small in numbers it was perhaps the most radical of the feminist groups. During the interwar years and during the war itself members worked on the campaign for equal compensation for war injuries and the campaign for equal pay (Newsome, 1957).

It was the Women's Freedom League, too, which led the feminist critique of the Beveridge Report in 1943. In its fortnightly bulletin it attacked the Beveridge conception of the man and wife as a team with the wife dependent on her husband for economic support. They also wanted women to pay the same contributions as men and to receive the same benefit. In November they held a conference drawing together a range of organizations in order to discuss objections to his scheme and in the following year a deputation of twelve women's organizations, led by the National Council of Women, went to meet the Ministry of Reconstruction to press their views, although without success (Wilson, 1977). The Women's Freedom League also published a critique of the Beveridge proposals, written by Elizabeth Abbott, founder of the Open Door Council, and K. Bompass. Arguing that Beveridge denied women their rights as persons, they were particularly critical of women's loss of insurance rights on marriage, and of all the contributions they had made prior to marriage (Clarke, Cochrane and Smart, 1987). In the general climate of support for Beveridge, however, the critique of these equal rights feminists went largely unnoticed, especially as many women welcomed his proposals (Dale and Foster, 1986).

By the end of the war some of the issues which had preoccupied the feminists in the 1920s and 1930s had been resolved. The marriage bar in teaching, which had been suspended during the war, was finally abolished by an amendment to the Education Act of 1944. Similarly, in 1946 the marriage bar in the civil service was abolished (Smith, 1986). Family allowances had also been approved by the government, although a vigorous campaign on the part of a number of women's organizations was necessary before they were paid to the mother (Stocks, 1949). The campaign for women police had also achieved many of its objectives by 1945 and the Women's Police Committee was disbanded (Carrier, 1988). Shortly after the war had ended the

British Nationality Act of 1948 allowed British women to keep their nationality on marriage (Carter, 1988).

The achievement of equal pay was however to prove more difficult since the Labour government of 1945, in spite of its support in principle, refused to implement the policy in practice. The main focus was on equal pay in the civil service and the major campaign body the Equal Pay Campaign Committee which had been founded in 1944. This group represented a number of feminist organizations, including the Six Point Group and the Open Door Council, and had the active support of a number of women in Parliament (Potter, 1957). Eventually a Conservative government gave equal pay to both teachers and civil servants in a series of instalments. This victory for the principle of equal pay applied to only a small proportion of women and not at all to industrial workers, but it was enough to bring the main thrust of the equal pay campaign to a close. The Equal Pay Committee went out of existence in 1956 and a few years later the feminist NUWT also disbanded, driven to this by the lack of recruits from the new generation of teachers (Pierotti, 1963). The Women's Freedom League also ceased to function in 1961 (Wilson, 1980; Pugh, 1992).

To some extent the closure of particular feminist groups may be explained in terms of the successful completion of several important feminist claims but there also seems to have been a general retreat from feminism during the postwar period which lasted well into the 1960s. The Abortion Law Reform Association, for example, founded in 1936, was in a serious state of decline by the 1950s. There appeared to be little public interest in the issue and it was not until the 1960s that the Association was revitalized by new recruits and by 1964 a new leadership (Hindell and Simms, 1971). The movement for the ordination of women, which had attracted considerable support from feminist groups, had been in decline since the 1930s and in the years after the war the issue seems to have aroused little interest even amongst feminists. It was not until the 1970s that the cause was reactivated as a result of the new women's movement (Heeney, 1988; Fletcher, 1989).

The movement for family endowment also came to a standstill as soon as family allowances were introduced, in spite of the fact that the scheme was inadequate in many ways. Indeed, there was no equivalent to the Family Endowment Society until the formation of the Child Poverty Action Group in 1965. In part this was due to the death, first of Eleanor Rathbone in 1946, and then of Eva Hubback in 1949, but other factors included the absence of any fears about a declining birth rate.

Low levels of unemployment also meant that there was also less anxiety about family poverty (Land, 1975; Macnicol, 1980). It seems likely in any case that even by the 1940s the feminist implications of family endowment had been submerged in other considerations.

The birth control movement had also by the 1950s become cautious and conservative in its approach. Although kept alive by the Family Planning Association, this had become largely a women's self-help enterprise. Avoiding the issue of women's rights, it also kept itself free from politics in order not to lose its charitable status. Moreover this situation did not really change until the issue of birth control was taken up by Labour women in the mid-1960s (Leathard, 1980).

There was also during this period a striking absence of new feminist groups. The main exception was the Married Women's Association but even this had been founded in 1938 by the Six Point Group. It was however important during the 1960s. Its aim was to promote the interests of the wife in the home so that it must be seen as an attempt on the part of the Six Point Group to include some aspects of the 'new' feminism in its programme. Its chief objective was to make marriage a financial partnership by giving wives a legal share in the family assets and it was concerned in particular with those wives without earnings or property of their own.

At first sight it appears to be an alternative to family endowment but there were many differences. For example, family endowment was always conceived as an extra payment to mothers with children and one of its aims was to mitigate, if not solve, the problem of family poverty as well as to give some recognition and even some financial independence to those women who were mothers. The aim of making marriage a financial partnership was to give women legal rights to assets acquired during marriage by virtue of their services to the household, and the campaign itself was fought on such issues as savings from the housekeeping and the right to a share in the marital home. It was therefore primarily an equal rights issue comparable with the issue of equal guardianship of children.

In trying to understand the mood within feminism in these years a sense of satisfaction with what had been achieved and a feeling of optimism about future progress were perhaps most important. This feeling of optimism, moreover, was already evident before the war. In 1936 a leading feminist, Ray Strachey, edited a collection of papers contributed by a number of leading figures in the women's movement. Although there were important variations, the general impression is one of satisfaction with what women had already achieved as a result of their emancipation through the vote. Indeed, Mary Hamilton, one of the earliest women Labour MPs, argued that women had already achieved equality in many fields, including politics. She accepted that economic inequality remained but thought this would be achieved through socialism rather than feminism (Strachey, 1936).

Elizabeth Wilson has argued that in the postwar period there was a widespread belief that women's oppression no longer existed and that women's problems had been solved. Even some feminists came to accept this view of things and Mary Stocks, for example, one of the leaders of NUSEC in the 1920s, felt able to write in 1970 'I am no longer a member of an unprivileged sex' (Stocks, 1970, p. 235). It is not surprising therefore to find the mood of feminism in the 1950s both cautious and conservative (Wilson, 1977). A report of a feminist conference, published in 1952, illustrates this remarkably well. Although taking the position that the feminist point of view should become more effective in public life and denying that marriage would or should absorb all the energies of an intelligent and educated woman for the whole of her life, it still took the view that a woman, even with a career, must continue to take responsibility for the domestic side of life and that this responsibility must come first. Indeed throughout the whole of the conference papers it is made very clear to the reader that not only the children's happiness but also that of the husband must be placed before the needs of a career. With this in mind girls are advised to choose a career which makes this possible and avoid any which might be too demanding. It is also emphasized very strongly that although there might be exceptions a woman's chief happiness comes from her home and family (Campbell, 1952).

A very similar position was taken up by Myrdal and Klein in their influential *Women's Two Roles*, published in 1956. Although feminist in its plea that women should have the choice of both marriage and career, it makes it clear that the duties of marriage and especially motherhood mean that work must always take second place in their lives (Myrdal and Klein, 1956). As Jane Lewis has pointed out, the absence of any radical reconstruction of either work or the family meant that women's proposed participation in paid employment was to be essentially in men's terms (Lewis, 1990).

This belief in women's 'dual role', in which a woman's work must somehow be made to fit into her domestic responsibilities, continued into the 1960s, even amongst feminists. For example, the Six Point

Group, in a pamphlet published as late as 1968, accepted the concept of the 'dual role' as the answer to women's problems (Six Point Group, 1968). Based on a conference investigating the success of the movement towards emancipation and the problems still remaining, it represented several different points of view and not necessarily the views of the Six Point Group itself. Nevertheless many of the contributors were surprisingly conservative for the late 1960s. Both of the contributors writing on home and employment, for example, accepted that a woman's domestic responsibilities had the prior claim.

In the 1920s Vera Brittain had been one of the most radical and outspoken of the 'equal rights' feminists, claiming for women exactly the same right to pursue a career as existed for men, even if that involved them in what she called a semi-detached marriage. To make a career an alternative to marriage was in her view wicked (Gorham, 1990; Berry and Bishop, 1985). Yet by the 1950s Vera Brittain herself, as we have seen, had retreated somewhat from the uncompromising equal rights feminism she was preaching as a young woman in the 1920s and 1930s. By 1953 she was no longer sure that feminism is about equal rights and placed more emphasis on changing men so that they become more like women, than on claiming for women the rights and privileges enjoyed by men (Brittain, 1953).

Part of the reason for this change lies in Brittain's involvement with Christian pacifism which led her to emphasize the differences between men and women and to value the qualities of love and toleration she saw as essentially female. She came indeed to accept the view that these differences were largely biological even though they had been reinforced by social structure, and even went so far as to argue that war violated a biological urge in women (Mellown, 1985). This is not to suggest that Brittain was no longer a feminist but rather that the nature of her feminism had now changed.

During the 1950s therefore there was a loss of confidence in the feminist goals of the 1920s and 1930s, and especially in women's right to independence whether this was seen in financial terms or in their right to a life of their own. Certainly if they were married they had no right to follow a career which threatened their prior responsibility to their husband and children. There was very little challenge even within feminism itself to an essentially biological view of women's needs, which argued that their chief happiness was to be found in their homes and families. Nor, perhaps for this reason, was there at this time any real challenge to the existing division of labour within the family.

By the 1960s, however, there is evidence that the mood was changing, although it is not until the 1970s that the distinctive arguments of
the modern feminist movement begin to be widely heard. At first there
was little more than a new mood of militancy, and a greater willingness even on the part of the more conservative women's organizations
to work with other groups. In 1962 for example the Townswomen's
Guild, which had always held aloof from other women's organizations, affiliated to the International Alliance of Women, and from this
time forward its links with other groups developed rapidly. When in
1968 Joyce Butler introduced a private member's bill to outlaw sex
discrimination they rallied to her support (Stott, 1978).

During the 1960s, too, there was growing support for changes in
family law to give greater protection to divorced and deserted wives, a
support which owed a great deal to the fear aroused by proposals not
only to make divorce easier but to make it possible for a man to
divorce his wife without her consent. When these proposals became
law in 1969 protest from a number of women's organizations forced
the Matrimonial Proceedings and Property Act, which modified the
law in the direction of giving wives a greater measure of financial
protection. Women's groups involved in this protest included the National Council of Women, the Federation of Business and Professional
Women's Clubs, and the Six Point Group (Stetson, 1982).

During the 1960s the Six Point Group, unlike the Women's Freedom
League, was still in existence, and from 1967 onwards it took an active
part in coordinating a variety of women's groups which cooperated
actively on a number of issues, particularly in the 1970s. Another very
active group at this time was the Fawcett Society, a development from
the Women's Employment Federation. A Status of Women group,
founded originally in the 1930s, was also reactivated in 1960 (Meehan,
1990). Moreover by the late 1960s the new feminism was beginning to
make itself heard. By 1969 there were already 70 local women's liberation groups in London alone (Meehan, 1990) and the first national
workshop was held in 1970.

In many respects this was a new movement with few links with the
older women's organizations. Indeed many of them not only held aloof
from it but felt alienated by much of its message. To some extent it had
different aims and certainly it had different methods of operation. It
was also much more radical than the old movement, more theoretical
and, above all, more confident. The caution of the 1950s was swept
away altogether. At the same time a new generation of young women

were brought into contact with feminist ideas and in the process the feminist movement was revitalized.

The present study, however, is concerned only with the period between 1918 and 1970. During these years, as this chapter has indicated, at no time can a feminist movement be said to have ceased to exist. There were always not only individual feminists but feminist groups working for feminist objectives. On the other hand these feminist groups never had the popular appeal, nor indeed the passion and commitment which characterized the suffrage movement, or in a different way the new women's movement of the 1970s. More surprising perhaps its history reveals neither a steady progress, nor a steady decline. Feminism was strongest perhaps in the 1920s, but the decline in the 1930s was followed by a fresh burst of activity at least on some fronts during the second world war. The postwar period, on the other hand, saw both the doubts and uncertainties of the 1950s, but also the resurgence of militancy in the 1960s, even before the new women's movement came on the scene.

It will be the aim of the second half of the study to try to explain these varying fortunes by setting them within a wider context. First however it will be necessary to examine women in the labour and trade union movement who for the purpose of clarity in the analysis have so far been neglected. Yet, as the next chapter will show, these women were also a significant part of feminist history, and have their own place in this study.

3. Women in the Labour Movement, and Feminism

In the previous chapter the groups described were not characterized simply by their feminism. They were also exclusively women's groups, organized by women and serving what were seen by their members as women's interests. A third characteristic was their autonomy, which gave them in effect complete independence, governed only by the wishes of their own members. The organizations which form the subject matter of the present chapter were also women's organizations but none of them saw themselves as serving only women's interests and none of them were completely autonomous, although in practice some had more independence than others. They were all part of a larger organization, controlled by men not women, in which women's needs did not necessarily play a part at all. This did not mean that women in the labour movement could not be feminists, and it is clear that some of them were, but it does mean that such women faced a constant conflict between their loyalty to feminism and their loyalty to the labour movement.

The earliest women's group within the Labour Party was the Women's Labour League. This was founded in 1906 with the purpose of encouraging support for the Party amongst women (Thane, 1990). Although at the start it was independent, in 1918 it became the Labour Party's women's section. Women's interests were also represented on the Party's executive committee by the appointment of four, later five, women members. Since, however, they were chosen by the annual conference of the Labour Party at which men were always in the majority, they represented the party as a whole and not its women members. An attempt to change this situation was made in 1921, when it was requested that the Labour women's conference rather than the annual conference should select the women representatives but this attempt was unsuccessful. The Labour women's conference, representing the women's sections, was itself only advisory but attempts from time to time to increase its power also failed (Smith, 1984b; Carter, 1988).

Perhaps the most influential body within the labour movement was the Standing Joint Committee of Industrial Women's Organizations, later the Joint Committee on Working Women's Organizations. Founded in 1916, it was formed from three groups, the Women's Labour League, the National Federation of Women Workers and the Women's Co-operative Guild. When the Women's Labour League became the women's section of the Labour Party, the four women on the Party's national executive, elected as we have seen by the annual conference, served on the standing committee, not women elected by the women's sections or by the women's conference. By 1923 it had incorporated a number of other bodies but all were associated with the labour and trade union movement.

If we turn now to look at the kind of policies advocated by both the SJC, as it came to be termed, and the women's sections we find that they have a great deal in common. Moreover both supported many of the issues which concerned feminist groups, described in the previous chapter. Equal pay, for example, was a common theme from 1918 onwards (Middleton, 1977; Thane, 1990) but support was also forthcoming from the labour women for those equal rights issues which were a dominant theme amongst the equal rights feminist groups. They included, for example, the married woman's right to work and the right of women to retain their British citizenship on marriage. Labour women also gave strong support to the 1920s birth control campaign (Soloway, 1982; Russell, 1977) and, from 1921, to the campaign for family endowment (Pedersen, 1989). During the 1930s the SJC also protested against discrimination against married women seeking unemployment benefit (Middleton, 1977).

Although sharing some of the concerns of the equal rights feminists, the labour women were much closer to the 'new' feminism of Eleanor Rathbone. Like the 'new' feminists they believed that most women would make marriage and motherhood their main preoccupation throughout their lives and their greatest need, therefore, was for an improvement in their lives within the home. For this reason they placed a great deal of emphasis on the need for safer maternal health and improved housing, as well as financial assistance to families, whether this took the form of family allowances or assistance in kind (Thane, 1990; Lewis, 1980).

There were, however, issues which divided the equal rights feminists and the labour women. There was, for example, a difference of opinion in 1919 when the Restoration of Pre-war Practices Act restored men's rights over certain jobs in industry. Lady Rhondda in a letter to the *Daily News* complained that the rights of women had been 'totally disregarded' (Adam, 1975, p. 73). Ray Strachey of the London Society for Women's Service actively lobbied against it. At this time NUSEC too was opposed although it later changed its mind. In 1920, however, Eleanor Rathbone, the new president, attacked it in her presidential address. Labour women, on the other hand, approved the Act as necessary and resented the attitude of women like Lady Rhondda (Smith, 1984b).

Even more important as a source of conflict was the issue of protective legislation which, as the previous chapter indicated, was opposed by all the equal rights feminists as hampering opportunities for women. Within the labour movement there was strong support and this was accepted by both SJC and the women's sections. (Thane, 1990; Alberti, 1989). NUSEC too had originally been in opposition but by 1926 there was a change of policy as many of NUSEC's leaders came to accept the labour and trade union movement's point of view. The Six Point Group continued in opposition, however, and feeling on the issue amongst equal rights feminists was strong enough to launch a new organization, the Open Door Council, specifically to argue against any protective legislation that was based on the sex of the workers rather than the nature of the work (Smith, 1990). To the equal rights feminists such legislation was founded on a belief in women's special vulnerability which was essentially false and they believed firmly that long hours and unhealthy conditions of work were equally harmful to both men and women.

The dispute over protective legislation was a source of controversy which drove a wedge between feminism and labour women for many years. In 1924, for example, Barbara Drake at the request of the SJC wrote a scathing attack on the feminists in the journal *Labour Women* (Drake, 1924). Later, in 1926, there was a pamphlet war on the issue between the SJC and the Open Door Council (Smith, 1990). The controversy was still in existence many years later and was probably one of the main reasons for the labour women's opposition to the Equal Citizenship (Blanket) Bill campaign during the war (Smith, 1986).

Undoubtedly, too, this difference of opinion on what both sides regarded as an important issue of principle was responsible for much of the hostility expressed by many labour women towards feminists and indeed feminism. This hostility was enhanced by their belief that feminism represented the interests of middle-class women rather than the women of the working classes, who were better served by the Labour Party. It is true that both the leadership and indeed much of the membership of the feminist groups was middle class and this was true even of the 'new' feminism of NUSEC, so that it is not difficult to understand the suspicion felt by the predominantly working-class labour women. In addition some at least of the campaigns waged by the feminists were of a kind to benefit mainly middle-class women. This was true for example of the attempt to open up the professions and the higher civil service to women, and even of the campaign for equal pay in the civil service and in teaching, although in both cases the principle involved was more generally applicable. There were also many other issues to do for example with the guardianship of children or with the maintenance of divorced and separated wives, which were as meaningful and perhaps sometimes more meaningful to working-class women.

Nevertheless, the resentment felt by labour women of what seemed to them the bourgeois nature of the feminist movement gave rise on a number of occasions to an outright refusal to cooperate with feminist groups, even when there were similar or common aims. In 1921, for example, the SJC declined to join the General Consultative Committee founded by Nancy Astor to coordinate the efforts of groups working to improve the status of women (Smith, 1984b). A similar hostility was shown to the Woman Power Committee set up during the early days of the war on the initiative of the British Federation of Business and Professional Women in association with a number of women MPs. Harold Smith suggests that this hostility seems to have been based on the fear that the Committee would seek preference for upper-class women in supervisory positions (Smith, 1984a). Moreover the SJC refused to join the Equal Compensation Campaign Committee in 1941 in spite of its full support of that body's aims which would in any case have also been of greater relevance to working-class women (Smith, 1981). A few years later there was a similar refusal to join the Equal Pay Campaign Committee set up by the Conservative MP Mavis Tate. Instead it set up its own campaign (Smith, 1981).

Although suspicion of what was perceived as an essentially bourgeois social movement was an important factor in the refusal of the

SJC to collaborate with feminist groups, another reason was more overtly political. It was the official labour view that labour women should not involve themselves in political organizations other than the Labour Party (Pugh, 1992), which disliked the attempt of the feminist groups to stand outside party politics. Although Labour Party supporters were not uncommon, especially in NUSEC, they joined the Party as individuals and none of the feminist groups aligned themselves with any of the political parties.

Labour leaders also tried to argue that feminism and the labour movement were incompatible (Smith, 1984b). They were totally opposed to the idea of women organizing on the basis of gender and tried to argue that class was more important than gender at least for working-class women. While accepting the idea of special women's representatives and special women's sections, both were kept very firmly under the control of the largely male-dominated Party organization. Although there were times when the women in the Party tried to assert their own point of view, they did on the whole accept that loyalty to the Party had to come first. Consequently although, as we have seen, labour women were themselves well aware of the significance of gender, their consciousness of loyalty to their class and their party held them aloof from those groups which were specifically organized around the issue of gender.

Although the loyalty of women in the Labour Party to its general principles was of considerable importance there were, nevertheless, times when issues of gender led to confrontation since some of the views expressed by labour women came into conflict with the attitudes of the party leadership. For several years during the 1920s the women's conference was overwhelmingly in support of allowing welfare centres to give birth control advice to women who were in need of it, but they were opposed by most of the Party leaders. Moreover the attitude of the male leadership was fully accepted by their Chief Woman Officer, Marion Phillips. Although pressure from the women's conference continued for several years they were unable to persuade the Party as a whole to accept their view. In 1929, indeed, they took the unusual step of turning to NUSEC, by this time converted fully to the birth control campaign, and the Workers' Birth Control and NUSEC formed a joint committee. In 1930, faced with pressure, not only from women's organizations but also from some local authorities, the Labour government allowed advice to be given if a woman's health was at risk, and this concession seems to have been sufficient to end controversy within the party.

The other main cause of disagreement between the women's section and the Party occurred on the issue of family endowment. The leadership of the Party, and especially the trade union movement, feared the effect of such schemes on wage negotiations but year after year the women's conference passed resolutions in favour of some form of family allowance. Instead of a family allowance paid to the mother, both the Labour Party and the TUC advocated widows' pensions, believing that in the ordinary course of events the father should be responsible for providing the income for the family. Various attempts were made to stifle the attempt on the part of the women's conference to campaign for family allowances and Pedersen suggests that Marion Phillips played a crucial role here as in the case of birth control, using her power as Chief Woman Officer to prevent the women's resolutions from getting on to the main agenda (Pedersen, 1989, p. 96). Not until the 1940s did family endowment become official Labour Party policy, and this change of policy had little to do with pressure from the women in the Party (Macnicol, 1980).

In the years after the second world war the main issue of contention between women and the Party was equal pay. It was the policy of the postwar Labour government not to implement equal pay at that time, and efforts were made, not altogether successfully, to stifle the protests of women in the Party. As in the prewar period use was made of the Chief Woman Officer, Mary Sutherland, to maintain discipline amongst the women in the Party. Arguing that there was no popular demand for it, she attempted to deflate criticism of the government's attitude (Meehan, 1990).

It also appears that, like the feminist groups, labour women's groups were in decline during the period after 1945. Not only did attendance at the women's conference fall during the 1950s (Pugh, 1992) but the Labour leadership and even women Labour MPs took little account of their deliberations. Nor did they generate distinctive policies as they had done in the 1920s, but tended on the whole to accept the orthodox Party lines. By the 1960s however there is evidence of a new mood of militancy among women in the Labour Party, not only on equal pay but on issues like discrimination against women, especially in employment, and the position of women in the system of social insurance and social security. By the mid-1960s moreover labour women were exerting strong pressure on the Labour Party to include family planning in the provisions of the National Health Service. Leathard suggests that they may have been prompted by guilt that abortion legislation had preceded free contraception (Leathard, 1980).

At the same time, a new chief woman officer was appointed in 1967 who was active in promoting the issue of equal rights within the Labour Party and who, therefore, formed an alliance with labour women rather than an alliance with the leadership of the Party against them. Indeed, it has been suggested that the 1975 anti-discrimination act was a victory for labour women who had worked for it continuously since the late 1960s (Carter, 1988). There is reason to believe that by this time the most sustained pressure for equal rights came from women in the Labour Party and not from the feminist organizations which, as the previous chapter suggested, had not yet recovered from the decline that had occurred in the 1950s.

Women in the Labour Party, however, comprised only one wing of the tripartite SJC and only one aspect of the labour movement. The Women's Co-operative Guild had been represented on the Committee since its foundation in 1916, by which time it was already well established as a highly active political group with its own individual programme. It was founded as part of the cooperative movement and served a dual purpose, since it attempted to further the cause not only of women but also of cooperation (Black, 1989). In that respect it was closer to the women's groups in the Labour Party than to the autonomous feminist organizations. Nevertheless, at least until the 1930s there is no doubt that it was strongly feminist in much of its policy even though, like the women in the Labour Party, it was a feminism which emphasized the needs of women as housewives and mothers. In the years both before and after the first world war there was an active commitment to an improvement in maternal and infant welfare and maternal health in particular was the subject of one of its most successful campaigns. It was also the issue of maternal mortality which led to its outspoken attitude during the interwar years to birth control and, more surprisingly, to abortion. In 1934, for example, its annual conference not only gave its overwhelming support to the legalization of abortion, but wanted an amnesty for women imprisoned as abortionists (Gaffin and Thoms, 1983).

Other feminist campaigns which occupied the Guild during these years included women magistrates and women police, issues which also involved a number of feminist groups during the 1920s in particular. They also supported the campaign for family allowances although, like the women in the Labour Party, they also emphasized the need for support in kind (Lewis, 1980). It was pacifism however which was the Guild's most distinctive feature. This reached its climax in the 1930s with its striking and original White Poppy Campaign. Even the outbreak of war did not shake its absolute commitment, although after some heart-searching it did become involved in a certain amount of welfare work. For example, during the London blitz it undertook to feed those families sheltering from the air raids in London's underground train system (Black, 1989).

In the years after the war the Guild's decline was swift. Its numbers fell dramatically and so did its commitment to feminism. During the war itself it still seems to have been quite active, taking part for example in the campaign to give compensation to housewives injured in the war. In 1943 it was involved in a campaign against the legal ruling that the housewife had no right to the savings from the housekeeping allowance. The Guild was also one of the groups which protested against the government's attempt to give family allowances to the father rather than the mother. By the 1950s, however, there was little sign of its prewar feminism, although its involvement in the very early days of the CND movement in 1955 and 1956 suggests that its pacifism still survived (Liddington, 1989).

Nevertheless, if the significance of the Guild to feminism did not survive the war, there is no doubt that in the years before the first world war and on into the period between the wars the Guild was a force to be reckoned with within the wider movement. Moreover, in spite of the fact that it was always part of the cooperative movement, and always regarded itself as such, the Guild was fiercely independent with respect to its policy. Indeed, for several years during the first world war the Guild lost its grant because of opposition within the cooperative movement to its liberal views on divorce. Its anti-war stand also brought it into conflict with the movement and Black suggests that this led to guildswomen being banned for several years from the Co-operative Party's list of possible Parliamentary candidates (Black, 1989).

At the same time, loyalty to the movement was very strong and effectively prevented any links between the Guild and the feminist groups, even when they had the same or similar aims. There were links with the rest of the labour movement through the Guild's membership of the SJC but it would not affiliate with any organization except those made up of working-class women in sympathy with the aims of the labour movement (Black, 1989). This effectively excluded all the non-Party feminist groups.

Nevertheless, the Guild was not able to gain for itself the position it clearly wanted within the cooperative movement. In spite of its firm belief that women, as housewives and consumers, had a very special contribution to make to the movement, and in spite too of the level of independence it had gained for itself, it was never able to achieve a significant place on the management committees of local societies, and had even less success at the higher levels. Its success should not, therefore, blind us to the fact that the cooperative movement, like the Labour Party, remained in the control of men. Nor does the Guild, like the women in the Labour Party, seem to have been particularly successful in converting the movement as a whole to its point of view. For men in the cooperative movement, as for men in the Labour Party, women's issues were at best irrelevant, at worst a dangerous distraction (Black, 1989).

Nor was there within the Guild the kind of feminist revival which occurred amongst labour women in the 1960s. There may have been a number of reasons for this, some associated with the decline of the Guild itself, some perhaps having their source in changes within the cooperative movement generally. In addition Black has suggested that the association of the new women's movement of the late 1960s with left-wing Labour politics helped to alienate women in the Guild who had little sympathy with this approach (Black, 1989). The heyday of the Guild was over by the 1950s, but in any history of the women's movement its earlier radicalism should not be forgotten.

The third wing of the SJC when it was founded in 1916 was the National Federation of Women Workers, an all-female organization led entirely by women. In 1917, however, it merged with the National Union of General Workers and from 1921 it became simply the women's section of that union. In order to represent women's interests within the trade union movement as a whole a special women's department was set up within the TUC and the TUC General Council included a women's group to represent unions that recruited women. Of the four places on this group, only two were reserved for women and the other two were and continued to be held by men. In 1927 the women's department was abolished and only a chief woman officer remained (Lewenhak, 1977; Boston, 1980). Perhaps the most important consequence of the loss of the National Federation of Women

Workers was that the number of women organizers dropped immediately (Lewis, 1984).

Clearly, therefore, not only were the interests of women trade unionists under-represented, but women themselves had little opportunity to meet together as women to debate the issues in which they had a particular interest. The General Council itself was almost entirely a male body and only a very small number of women ever attended the Trades Union Congress (Lewis, 1984). In consequence there were demands for a separate women's conference and this was formed in 1925 as a purely advisory group, its main aim to develop ways of recruiting women into unions (Soldon, 1978; Lewenhak, 1977). In 1931 a national women's advisory group was formed. Although an all-women's group, its functions were limited and Lewenhak has suggested that by the late 1930s it had become very much part of the trade union establishment with a strong commitment to the political side of the movement.

During the 1920s and 1930s the demands of women trade unionists, like those of women in the Labour Party, focused on improvements in maternity and child services (Boston, 1980). There was however some opposition in the 1930s to the lack of national insurance provisions for married women (Smith, 1986). During the war equal pay and equal compensation became important issues as they did for other women's organizations (Boston, 1980). Another wartime issue was the provision of day nurseries for mothers at work (Summerfield, 1984). Like women in the Labour Party the women in the trade union movement strongly supported protective legislation, and during the war they opposed the Equal Citizenship (Blanket) Bill proposed by the Six Point Group because of its effect on such legislation (Smith, 1986).

In the years following the second world war support for day nurseries, which had been largely a temporary wartime measure, declined (Riley, 1983). By the 1950s however there was growing concern among women trade unionists at the lack of nursery provision in spite of little interest in the trade union movement as a whole (Boston, 1980). The TUC General Council, including its women members, wanted factory-run nurseries on the ground that they were the responsibility of industry not the government. In 1953, for example, Anne Godwin, a Council member, argued that there was no obligation to maintain the children of women who go out to work (Birmingham Feminist History Group, 1979). Others believed that women with young children should not be at work at all. By 1957, however, the situation had changed. In that year, in response to repeated resolutions and speeches at the women's advisory conference, the National Advisory Committee withdrew its opposition to day nurseries for working mothers with young children (Lewenhak, 1977).

The issue of greatest concern during the postwar years was however not day nurseries but equal pay and this too led to controversy between the conference delegates and the TUC leadership. As we have seen earlier in this chapter the postwar Labour government was determined to resist demands for equal pay until they judged the time to be ripe for it. Accordingly pressure was applied within the trade union movement as within the Labour Party itself. In 1948, for example, Florence Hancock, a woman trade union leader, appealed to the delegates to put economic needs first (Lewenhak, 1977). During the following years attempts by the General Council to control the women's conference increased and more resolutions were opposed by the platform. The TUC leadership, male and female, not only supported the appeals of the government in the face of inflation, but there was also a preference in some quarters for achieving equal pay by wage negotiation rather than by government legislation. However there was little pressure by trade union negotiators, who were mainly men, for equal pay, and during this period wage increases for male workers often widened the gap between the pay of men and women (Boston, 1980).

During the 1950s, nevertheless, there were clear signs of a more militant mood among women trade unionists, and by the end of the decade this militancy began to have an effect. In 1963, suggestions for a TUC women's charter included equal pay, better promotion opportunities, apprenticeship provisions for girls, better training facilities, and better provisions for health and welfare. By 1968 women's growing impatience within both the trade unions and the Labour Party led to a National Joint Action Campaign Committee for Equal Rights. By 1970 the TUC General Council was itself prepared to back the women's demands and, with a Labour government in power, the way was prepared for the Equal Pay Act of 1970 (Lewenhak, 1977).

In spite of this success, however, there is no doubt that women in the trade union movement were seriously hindered by their lack of any real power within the movement as a whole. They had only a token representation on the important General Council of the TUC, and the women's conference was never more than an advisory body. The women's advisory committee also had no power to do more than give advice, and, as we have seen, there were times when it seemed more anxious to keep the conference delegates in line with official TUC and sometimes government policy than to allow them to express an opposition view. In this respect the committee seems to have played a similar role to the chief woman officer in the Labour Party.

If we turn now to look at the position of women within individual trade unions their lack of power is perhaps even more in evidence. Not only did some craft unions exclude women altogether but even in mixed unions few women held an official position and, indeed, during the 1920s and 1930s the number actually decreased as women officers died or resigned (Soldon, 1978). Not until the late 1950s did this tendency change as more women began winning elections (Lewenhak, 1977). Within mixed unions, moreover, women were frequently confined to special sections, paying lower contributions and getting lower benefits (Lewis, 1984). This domination on the part of male members was true not only of manual worker unions but white-collar unions too. Even the National Union of Teachers, with a considerable majority of women members, was almost entirely controlled by men. Not only were very few women elected to the national executive committee but the majority of delegates at national conferences were men (Partington, 1976). The Burnham Committee, which decided on teachers' pay, also had a large majority of male members (Oram, 1987).

It is not altogether surprising, therefore, to find the NUT less than enthusiastic in its attitude to feminist issues like equal pay and the marriage bar. There is evidence, too, that male teachers were, before the first world war, openly hostile to demands by women members for both equal pay and women's suffrage (Pierotti, 1963). Equal pay was also rejected by the annual conference in 1917. In 1919, however, a referendum which was able to reflect the views of women members and not just those, mostly men, who attended the conference brought a resounding victory for equal pay with 35 004 in favour and only 15 059 against. A year later however an anti-equal pay motion was again passed by the annual conference.

Faced with a clear difference between male and female attitudes but faced, too, with the desire to keep both men and women in the union, the NUT continued to hedge on the issue, failing to press equal pay in its negotiations but unwilling to argue against it. Indeed, not until the last stages of the equal pay campaign in the early 1950s did the NUT come out strongly in support, along with other mixed white-collar unions like the National Association of Local Government Officers and the Civil Service Clerical Association (Partington, 1976).

The situation was further complicated by the breakaway of the National Association of Schoolmasters in 1919 and the National Union of Women Teachers in 1920. Although other issues were involved, differences over equal pay were the main factor in the case of both breakaway unions. Indeed the National Association of Schoolmasters was an implacable opponent of equal pay until the end of the campaign in the 1950s. The National Union of Women Teachers (NUWT) was, as the previous chapter indicated, as much a feminist group as a trade union, cooperating with other feminist organizations on a wide variety of issues. They campaigned, for example, not only for greater opportunities for women teachers, but against gender-differentiated education and the traditional sexual division of labour (King, 1987).

The need to keep the allegiance of its male members also dictated the NUT's attitude to the marriage bar. Introduced into teaching in the 1920s in order to deal with the large number of young women who had qualified as teachers but could not find work because of cuts in education spending, the marriage bar was nevertheless seen as a feminist issue because of its denial of the married woman's right to work. For this reason it was of considerable importance to a large number of feminist groups, and was of particular relevance to the NUWT. As in the case of equal pay, however, the attitude of the NUT was ambiguous. Although resolutions against the marriage bar were carried at each NUT annual conference from 1924 to 1927, the union itself seems to have been divided on the issue and sometimes local union officials were in support of the bar (London Feminist History Group, 1983).

Although it undoubtedly had the support of the Board of Education, the policy itself was initiated by local education authorities and it was indeed quite possible for a local authority to refuse to implement it at all. In Manchester, for example, it was brought to an end in 1928 by a campaign led by Shena Simon. There was also a considerable variation in the severity with which it was imposed. In Rhondda, for example, all married women teachers were summarily dismissed even though it meant in some cases the loss of pensions by teachers of almost pensionable age. In spite of the hardship to the teachers involved the NUT refused to support them in their legal battle with the local education authority and the teachers were forced to finance themselves. On the other hand the NUT was prepared to support the teachers at Poole and, after some pressure, took part in a deputation to the Board of Education in 1927. None of the cases actually succeeded, although in Poole the NUT won the first round only to lose on appeal. It was the NUWT therefore which carried the brunt of the campaign. Apart from numerous deputations, it sponsored the election of Agnes Dawson to the LCC to work for the removal of the bar and her efforts helped to get it lifted in London in 1935 (Pierotti, 1963).

Another area in which the attitude of the NUT contrasted strongly with that of the NUWT was the headship of mixed schools. The National Association of Schoolmasters took the view that men teachers should not under any circumstances have to serve under a woman and this effectively precluded a woman headmistress in any but a school with an all female staff. As the number of mixed schools was increasing during this period an attitude of this kind seriously harmed women teachers' promotion prospects and the NUWT fought strenuously against it. The NUT on the other hand, in spite of an official policy on equal opportunities for men and women, acquiesced in the policy generally adopted by local authorities that the heads of mixed schools should always be men. The NUT was also inclined to accept the view, put forward by the National Association of Schoolmasters, that older boys should be taught by men (Oram, 1987, 1989).

Another white-collar union, the Civil Service Clerical Association, was also ambiguous in its attitudes to feminist issues. Moreover, like the teachers, the civil servants had their own breakaway union, the all-female National Federation of Women Civil Servants, which like the NUWT was an outspoken feminist organization. Indeed, in the period immediately after the first world war the equal pay fight was carried on almost entirely by these two unions. Like the NUT, on the other hand, the CSCA came fairly late into the picture so far as the equal pay campaign was concerned and when this occurred it had more to do with the increase in the number of low-paid women clerks, brought in to do men's jobs, than with any commitment to feminist principles on the part of the male clerks. As Lewenhak points out, equal pay was seen mainly as protection for men's prior right to jobs and it is not surprising to find some women anxious that equal pay might be a threat to their jobs. When the issue was debated at the National Association of Local Government Officers' conference, for example, women delegates spoke against equal pay in both 1932 and 1936 for precisely that reason (Lewenhak, 1977). By the late 1930s however most of the mixed white-collar unions were moving towards support for equal pay and were an important element in major equal pay campaigns both during and after the war (Potter, 1957).

The marriage bar was another area in which the whole-hearted opposition of the National Federation of Women Civil Servants contrasted with opposition from the mixed Civil Service Clerical Association. Indeed, the CSCA actually lobbied against the 1927 Bill, sponsored by NUSEC to end the marriage bar, an opposition which was tellingly exploited by the opponents of the Bill. A ballot on the marriage bar showed a majority of union members in opposition and it is clear that women, as well as men, saw married women as a threat to their jobs. Nevertheless there is evidence of a considerable gender difference in attitudes. Women's unions tended to oppose the bar and this was true not only of the NUWT and the National Federation of Women Civil Servants but also of the Association of Women Clerks and Secretaries (Boston, 1980). Moreover, when in 1935/6 the LCC Staff Association held a referendum on the marriage bar, over two-thirds of all those voting, including both men and women, wanted the bar retained, but of the women voters the proportion was only two-fifths and therefore a majority of women wanted it lifted (Lewenhak, 1977).

In attempting to sum up the relationship between women in the trade union movement and feminism it is clear that, although like other women in the labour movement they held aloof from feminist groups, they did nevertheless share a number of feminist goals. Their women's charter, proposed in 1963, for example included not only equal pay but better opportunities for both training and promotion. There was also a demand for nursery school provision for the children of working mothers. Like other labour women however there was a strong commitment to protective legislation which was an important element in their opposition to equal rights feminism. It would also appear that trade union women did not share in the emphasis on the housewife and mother which characterized women in the Labour Party women's sections and the Women's Co-operative Guild. This undoubtedly reflects their experience as working women, and increasingly by the 1960s as working wives and working mothers. Thus although sharing a commitment to the wider labour and trade union movements, the trade union women represented a view of feminism which, in spite of their difference of opinion on protective legislation, was closer to equal rights feminism than to the 'new' feminism which tended to see women primarily, if not indeed only, as housewives and mothers.

On the other hand, women trade unionists were seriously hampered by their lack of power within the trade union structure, which left all the major policy decisions in male hands. Although they were allowed their own conference, it was strictly advisory, as was the women's advisory committee. At the level of individual unions, too, decisions were in the hands of the male members who, even in unions with many female members, held the majority of official positions and formed the majority at annual conferences. Unions like the NUWT tried to avoid this situation by forming a breakaway women's union but this was not necessarily an advantage in the long run. Such unions could, it is true, make their own policy but they appealed to only a minority of women and, however lively, remained unable to influence either public policy or the policies of the parent union.

Women in the trade union movement also suffered because like labour women generally they owed loyalty to a wider movement that did not share many of their goals. Male trade unionists were not feminists and this was true at all levels, but most especially at the shop-floor level where there was often outright hostility to women's demands for equal pay and better promotion opportunities. In consequence women in the trade union movement as in the Labour Party not infrequently found themselves in opposition to their leadership. Moreover when such disagreements occurred it was not unusual for women trade union leaders, motivated certainly by loyalty to the wider movement, to take what might be described as the establishment view. This was true, for example, with respect to the Restoration of Pre-War Practices Act of 1919, which was supported unequivocally by women like Mary McArthur, and it was also true of equal pay at the end of the second world war.

Clearly, therefore, this conflict of loyalty was a problem for women in the labour and trade union movements in coming to terms with issues of gender. Whatever their commitment to the goals of the wider movement, and this was often high, on the issue of gender they and the wider movement were all too frequently out of step. Yet, as we have seen, in spite of important differences women in the labour and trade union movements, and in the Women's Co-operative Guild, had a great deal more in common with the feminist groups than is generally realized or indeed than they, perhaps, realized themselves. Cut off from feminist groups for reasons of class and politics, they did share a commitment to gender as an issue which not only allied them, ideologically at least, with feminism but also brought them into conflict with many, if not most, of the men in the movements.

Although therefore their position within the labour movement disadvantaged labour women in their campaigns on behalf of their gender, it does not necessarily follow that the path chosen by the autonomous feminist groups was the more advantageous for feminism. Although undisturbed by the conflicts of loyalty that beset labour women, they were never more than small and frequently ineffective pressure groups, working outside the political process. The labour women, in contrast, whatever their problems with the wider movement, were nevertheless insiders and as such did exercise a degree of influence on politics which was not easily available to feminist pressure groups.

It was, however, women in Parliament who, potentially at least, held the greatest power, since they were part of the political process itself. At the same time, with the exception of Independent MPs – and only one during the whole period held such a position – their involvement in party politics was virtually total. The only way for them to enter Parliament at all was through a party machine, and once elected they were held rigidly by party discipline as well as by loyalty to the party of their choice. This party loyalty also acted to divide women MPs from each other, so that any attempt to unite on issues of gender necessarily had to cut across party divisions within the House. The following chapter looks specifically at women MPs and examines their relationship both to the women's movement and to party politics.

4. Women in Parliament

There have been several studies of women in Parliament (Harrison, 1986; Vallance, 1979; Brookes, 1967; Pugh, 1992), although none of them have dealt specifically with their relationship to feminism. The conclusion, which has generally been drawn from these studies, is that women MPs have had very little interest in women's issues and, indeed, Vallance has argued that they have with only a few exceptions seen themselves as MPs who happen to be women rather than as women MPs. Certainly there is truth in this judgement but the exceptions were by no means as rare as Vallance suggests and, although women MPs did not often collaborate across party lines women from different parties shared a similar attitude to women's issues. It will be the argument of this chapter that women MPs made more of a contribution to feminism than is sometimes supposed.

Brian Harrison has demonstrated that for the period up to 1945, at least, women MPs on the whole devoted relatively little of their debating contribution to women's issues and this is true even of such a committed feminist as Nancy Astor. Nevertheless this did not necessarily indicate a lack of interest in such matters. The Parliamentary agenda was, and still is, set not by individual MPs but by the two main political parties and, in particular, by the party in power. Since neither the Conservatives nor the Labour Party was prepared to give priority to women's issues, women – and indeed men as well – who wanted to bring such issues before the House of Commons were forced to resort mainly to questions to ministers or, if they were lucky in the ballot, to private member's bills. On some occasions amendments to a government bill could be used in this way and indeed were used with some effect from time to time, as this chapter will show, but even if such an amendment were successful in the House it could still be defeated by the government, or by the House of Lords.

It is true, of course, that women MPs rarely operated as a group, divided as they were by party allegiance and party discipline. As Harrison has pointed out, political preferment was dependent on working with the grain of the party, so that acts of party disloyalty could have quite serious consequences. Nevertheless, this loyalty could sometimes be severely strained and at times even broken. These occasions are of particular importance when they occurred, as they did from time to time, on issues of gender.

In focusing in this chapter on women in Parliament it must be emphasized that issues of gender were not of interest only to women MPs. A number of male MPs were involved too, and indeed had been involved throughout the whole period of the struggle for women's suffrage. On all the main issues fought by women MPs for women during the period reviewed here there were men prepared to work for the same goals, even if their motives were sometimes very different. Indeed, without male support the small number of women in Parliament would have been completely ineffectual. Unlike the political parties, which could and did rely on numbers, women in Parliament had to rely on persuasion.

It was on the issue of equal pay that the unity among women MPs was most obvious and most forceful. One of the reasons for this was the long period of struggle to achieve this aim and the persistence of the opposition to it. Indeed, although some women achieved equal pay in 1955 there was no general legislation until 1970 and then only in a form which was subsequently shown to be highly unsatisfactory. The campaign for equal pay therefore lasted throughout the whole period of this study, and in some respects at least played an equivalent role to the suffrage campaign in uniting the women's movement. Although some women, like Eleanor Rathbone for example, had doubts about equal pay, especially without a system of family allowances, it was a goal which united both feminists and labour women throughout the whole of the period, in spite of some fears that it might lead to some loss of jobs for women.

In the House of Commons, in spite of the individual exceptions, there was also strong support for equal pay from women whatever their party. It was also, despite strong and persistent opposition at the level of the government, an issue which commanded considerable support from male MPs and this again was true irrespective of party. At first the issue was raised mainly in connection with the civil service, since this was seen as an area of employment directly under government control, and the civil service continued to remain at the centre of the Parliamentary campaign for many years. Major Hills, a Conservative MP, was one of the most persistent campaigners not only for equal pay in the civil service but also for equal conditions of entry and employment, and during the years from 1920 to 1924 the issue was raised on a number of occasions both by Major Hills and by other MPs, both men and women (Hansard, 19 May 1920, 5 August 1921, 6 August 1924).

At this time however not only were there very few women in Parliament, but they were concerned with a number of other feminist issues and equal pay does not seem to have been of central concern to them, as indeed it does not seem to have been to women's groups outside Parliament. Indeed, it was not until 1936 that equal pay began to take the centre of the stage. In April of that year Ellen Wilkinson, a Labour MP, introduced a motion on equal pay in the civil service (Hansard, 1 April 1936). It was opposed by two women MPs, Eleanor Rathbone and the Duchess of Atholl on the ground of the family responsibilities of the male workers. The Duchess of Atholl was a Conservative, who had on more than one occasion during the 1920s argued against the extension of women's suffrage but Eleanor Rathbone, an Independent, was one of the most outspoken feminists in the House of Commons who contributed more on women's issues than any other woman MP during this period (Harrison, 1986), so that their alliance was an unusual one. Nevertheless, Rathbone was not prepared to vote against the motion and the Duchess of Atholl was the *only* woman to vote with the government in opposition to the motion.

At this time, of course, a Conservative government was in power and this presented the Conservative women with particular problems, solved by some by the decision not to vote at all. This did not, however, necessarily reflect their view on the issue itself, and two of them, Irene Ward and Mavis Tate, were in subsequent years among the most vigorous of equal pay supporters in Parliament. Other Conservative women, including Nancy Astor, felt strongly enough to vote against their own government and in defiance of the government whip. Interestingly, the mood of the House, in spite of the Conservative majority, was with the motion, and it was carried although with only a small majority. At this stage the Prime Minister intervened and asked for the support of the House as a matter of confidence. Faced with such an ultimatum the House reversed the vote and this time the motion was lost substantially (Hansard, 6 April 1936). Nevertheless, if on this occasion party loyalty was the victor, there is little doubt that in the final voting most of the women in the House were forced to vote against their own convictions.

In the following years equal pay was never long absent from discussion in the House of Commons, and the issue gained increasing importance during the war as more and more women were involved in some form of war service. In 1939, for example, a Conservative MP, Mavis Tate, raised both unequal allowances for men and women in the Air Raid Precautions Service and inequality between men and women in naval and military pensions (Hansard, 2 March 1939). Later in the year Jenny Adamson, one of the few Labour women in the House at that time, queried the Personal Injuries (Emergency Provisions) Act, under which wives not gainfully employed were not allowed any compensation for injuries, although husbands were entitled to an allowance if their wives were incapacitated. She also questioned the difference in compensation allowed to *single* men as compared with *single* women. She was seconded by another Labour MP, Edith Summerskill, and supported by another Labour MP, Ellen Wilkinson. The House divided on the issue but the motion was lost. The Conservative women voted with them, except for those who abstained rather than voting against the motion (Hansard, 24 October 1939).

Although the motion was lost the subject itself was not dropped. Edith Summerskill raised the issue early in 1941 (Hansard, 22 January 1941), and two Conservative MPs, Mavis Tate and Irene Ward, in February (Hansard, 13 February 1941). They were told that the Minister of Pensions had received deputations from women's organizations and 'lady members of the House' and that the case was under consideration. By this time, indeed, interest in the issue had increased enormously both inside and outside Parliament. Several Conservative women were now involved, and although Edith Summerskill remained active, the leadership now passed to Mavis Tate. A lengthy debate in March involved a large number of MPs (Hansard, 20 March 1941), and in May Mavis Tate moved to annul the 1939 Act, seconded by Edith Summerskill. In the voting that followed the motion, which was opposed by the coalition government, was defeated but no women voted against it (Hansard, 1 May 1941).

In the months that followed the campaign continued to gain momentum with petitions submitted from both Edith Summerskill (Labour) and Mavis Tate (Conservative). Indeed it attracted more support than the equal pay campaign itself, probably because the issue was not just between men and women but between single men and single women. Men with dependents were given extra allowances so that arguments based on a man's greater family responsibilities, which both men and women found persuasive, were no longer relevant. It was also very much a women's campaign. In the House of Commons the opposition came only from men. Women MPs, whatever their party, rallied in support. In November, 1942 Mavis Tate and Edith Summerskill both raised the issue in the debate on the address and when the matter was pressed to a vote the government suffered a sharp defeat with only 95 MPs in their favour and 229 against. All the women backbenchers voted for the motion and only three women, all of whom were holding government positions, abstained (Hansard, 25 November 1942).

The government itself was clearly shaken by this defeat and it offered a select committee on the issue of compensation, although carefully excluding any consideration of equal pay in general from its discussions. A year later the committee reported in favour of equal compensation for single men and women, and the government at last gave way, although it was made clear in the House that the new rates applied only to compensation for war injuries and not to any other form of sex discrimination (Hansard, 7 April 1943). Indeed the determined opposition of the government to equal compensation was certainly an attempt to avoid any wider discussion of equal pay which they were quite determined to thwart except in the very limited circumstances in which women had taken on, temporarily, jobs formerly held only by men. Moreover this opposition to any pressure for equal pay was held by both Labour and Conservative leaders within the wartime coalition (Smith 1981).

With the equal compensation campaign successfully concluded, however, a number of women MPs turned to the wider issue of equal pay. Early in January 1944 an Equal Pay Campaign Committee had been set up under the leadership of Mavis Tate who was its chairman (sic) until her death in 1947. Another prominent member was Thelma Cazalet-Keir, also a Conservative MP, who served as chairman from 1947 until the committee's dissolution in 1956. Thelma Cazalet-Keir had been prominent in the campaign for equal compensation and in 1944, in the House of Commons, she moved an amendment to the Education bill then under discussion, to grant equal pay to teachers. The Minister of Education, Butler, opposed on the ground that the salaries of teachers were the concern of the Burnham Committee and not the government, but his argument did not convince the House of Commons and Cazalet-Keir's amendment was carried although by only one vote. There were no women amongst those who opposed it (Hansard, 28 March 1944).

In spite of the Commons' vote the government continued to insist that they could not accept the amendment. Instead, Churchill intervened, supported strongly by Bevin, and the issue, as in 1936, was made one of confidence in the government. Many of the women MPs were angered by his action but it had the desired effect. Very few MPs were prepared to overthrow the government in wartime and Cazalet-Keir, a committed feminist but a loyal Conservative and an admirer of Churchill, told the House that she had no choice but to vote against her own amendment. Others followed her example and the vote in favour dropped from 117 to 28, so that the amendment was defeated. The only two women MPs who felt able to challenge the government were Agnes Hardie and Edith Summerskill, both members of the Labour Party (Hansard, 29 March 1944).

Two months later, in reply to a question on equal pay from Cazalet-Keir, the Prime Minister announced the setting up of a Royal Commission, but this was a delaying tactic on the part of a government determined to avoid the issue of equal pay, although frightened by the level of support in the House. Not only was the actual setting up of the Commission deliberately delayed but it was told that it must gather facts and not make recommendations. It had the required effect nevertheless and the campaigners held their fire in order to wait for the Commission's report.

In 1945 a Labour government came into power with a large majority and the composition of the House of Commons was dramatically changed. Several Conservative women, active in the equal pay campaign, were no longer in the House but the number of Labour women had increased considerably, many of them equally committed to equal pay. The Labour government was, however, just as adamant in its opposition to equal pay as the coalition government had been. In spite of a resolution calling for its immediate implementation, carried by 2 310 000 votes to 598 000 at the 1947 Labour Party conference, the government flatly refused to put this resolution into effect. Although forced to admit that it was Labour Party policy, at least in principle, it argued that for reasons of cost no immediate implementation was possible. Indeed, Labour leaders like Hugh Dalton and Stafford Cripps were opposed to discussing even its introduction in the future (Lewenhak, 1977).

Labour MPs were therefore forced to attack their own government if they pressed hard for equal pay, and a number were clearly inhibited by the government's attitude. Several newly elected Labour women did however raise the issue in Parliament in the period 1945–50, including Barbara Castle, Leah Manning, Barbara Ayrton Gould and Elaine Burton. There is some evidence that the government deliberately tried to muzzle its own supporters at this time and, according to Jean Mann, the new Labour MPs were instructed to keep quiet and to vote the government's legislation through (Pugh, 1992, p. 308). In 1950 the government was decidedly equivocal towards equal pay at the International Labour Office conference that year and were forced to defend themselves as best they could in the House of Commons (Hansard, 11 July 1950, 2 November 1950). By 1951 however the government's attitude against equal pay seems to have hardened. In June of that year a statement from Gaitskell in reply to a deputation from the staff side of the Whitley Council went further than any previous statement, raising not only the question of cost, but also the familiar, though incorrect, argument that 'the majority of men' had dependent families (Hansard, 20 June 1951). In August, with Labour still in power, Labour MP, Douglas Houghton brought forward a motion in his name, signed by 70 Members from both parties. He was answered by Douglas Jay who reiterated Gaitskell's claim that the average male earner was a husband and father (Hansard, 2 August 1951).

The return of a Conservative government in 1951 gave further impetus to the demand for equal pay which came from both sides of the House. In May there was a debate, initiated again by Douglas Houghton, and he was supported by a large number of women from both parties. Indeed there was a close association between Barbara Castle and the Conservative, Irene Ward, and Barbara Castle led an all-party deputation to the minister. The pull of party loyalty was still strong however and Barbara Castle reported to the House that she had been criticized by some of her women colleagues because of this collaboration across party lines (Hansard, 16 May 1952). The arguments were received sympathetically by the Conservative minister, Boyd Carpenter, in sharp contrast to the attitude of the previous Labour government, and he promised that steps would be taken to implement equal pay in the public services within the lifetime of the existing government.

In the following two years pressure on the minister continued. Finally, in March 1954, a bill was moved by Douglas Houghton and signed by nearly 200 MPs from both sides of the House (Hansard, 9 March 1954). In May the government announced that negotiations were in progress with the Whitley Council and details were made public by Butler in January 1955. However he specifically excluded the industrial civil service and, by implication, all women working in industry (Hansard, 27 January 1955). Later, teachers were added to the scheme but there was no legislation for women in manual work until 1970.

More surprisingly, most of the pressure for equal pay ended, at least temporarily, with the granting of equal pay to teachers and to non-industrial civil servants. This was partly because it was the white-collar unions who were most pressing in their claims and partly because their claims had been accepted by the Royal Commission in its report in 1946, although the claims of women industrial workers had been denied on the ground that they were less efficient than male workers. The Labour Party, moreover, had pledged itself to equal pay by the 1960s although, once in office, there were delays in its implementation due to the imposition of a wages freeze. In 1968 Barbara Castle, now Minister of Labour, set up a working party specifically to prepare the way for equal pay legislation and Hattersley reiterated that in spite of the delay it was still government policy (Hansard, 6 May 1965). When the government bill was finally introduced in 1970 it was passed without a division.

There is no doubt therefore that there was considerable support amongst women MPs for the principle of equal pay. Moreover, this support did not follow party lines and active equal pay campaigners in the House might belong to either of the two main parties. Although it was rare for a woman to vote against her own party, the tactic of abstention was frequently brought into play and there were a number of occasions when loyalty to the principle of equal pay overcame their party loyalty so that they voted against their own government. One further point to notice, in so far as the equal pay campaign is concerned, is that women MPs did not, on the whole, have to face a hostile House of Commons. There was a strong body of support amongst the men in the House, even if, for some of them at least, their reasons had more to do with the elimination of competition from women at work than with justice to women. The main obstacle to success was not the House of Commons but the government which, for a variety of reasons, remained adamantly opposed to granting equal pay, even when they claimed to accept it in principle. This was a situation which changed only when a Conservative government accepted equal pay in the civil service and teaching in 1955. The resistance of governments to equal pay is however of considerable significance and will be discussed in detail in subsequent chapters.

No other feminist issue occupied the attention of women MPs in quite the same way or indeed for so long a period. There were nevertheless long-running campaigns which were issues of gender rather than party, and which did enjoy widespread support amongst women MPs. One of the most interesting of these, because it had been among some of the earliest feminist goals, was the claim for equal guardianship rights for men and women. The law on guardianship had been amended twice in the nineteenth century but the position when women first entered Parliament was still grossly unequal. New legislation was sought as early as 1921 when a bill, sponsored by NUSEC with support from several other women's organizations, was introduced by Colonel Greig, a Liberal, and seconded by Nancy Astor (Hansard, 6 May 1921). The bill passed its second reading and was not unsympathetically received by the government but no further action was taken. In 1924 another bill was introduced by Margaret Wintringham and was actively supported by the women in the House. Even the Duchess of Atholl, not normally sympathetic to feminist claims, spoke in its support and no woman MP opposed it (Hansard, 4 April 1924). The bill was committed to a standing committee but was considered by the then Labour government to be too controversial and they introduced a compromise bill of their own, but the dissolution of Parliament then intervened. Eventually, in 1925, substantially the same bill was introduced by the Conservatives. In the new bill a mother was granted equal guardianship only when the marriage was at an end either by a divorce or a legal separation, so that while a marriage was in being the father still remained the legal guardian. The purpose of the compromise was to preserve the household as a single unit which, the government and its supporters believed, would be threatened if husband and wife were given equal rights (Smith, 1990; Brophy, 1982).

Although the new Act did not concede the principle of the original bill, it did remove some of the worst grievances and for this reason it was accepted as the compromise it was by women in the House. Ellen Wilkinson, for example, supported the bill although she complained that it did not go far enough (Hansard, 4 March 1925). There was also some discontent among women's organizations at the loss of the original bill (Brophy, 1982). Nevertheless it was not until 1962 that further attempts were made to improve on the 1925 Act. In that year Joan Vickers, a Conservative, introduced a new bill to bring some improvement in the guardianship rights of mothers (Hansard, 7 March 1962). When nothing came of this bill she introduced a second bill in 1965 (Hansard, 7 April 1965). This passed its second reading and went to a standing committee but made no further progress. Finally, in 1973 a government bill gave genuine guardianship rights to both parents (Hansard, 8 May 1973). A Conservative measure, it was part of a pledge in the election manifesto to remove discrimination against women in law.

Another legal issue which concerned women MPs of both parties was the loss of British nationality which occurred when a woman married a foreigner. This was raised in the House of Commons in 1922 when a bill, seconded by Nancy Astor, passed without a division but was rejected by the House of Lords. A further attempt was made in 1925, again seconded by Nancy Astor and passed without a division, but was rejected by the government on the ground that they could do nothing without the consent of the self-governing dominions (Hansard, 18 February 1925). In 1930 Ethel Bentham, a Labour MP, moved the second reading of a nationality bill, supported by three other women, one Conservative and two Labour. The Labour Party was now in office but, although they gave their support in principle, once more the government raised the issue of the self-governing dominions. Nevertheless, it did offer a government bill to help those women threatened with statelessness and in time of war (Hansard, 28 November 1930).

The promised government bill was eventually introduced in 1933 under the National Coalition government which replaced Labour. It was applicable to women who had become stateless and because it did offer a measure of relief in these cases it was accepted in this spirit. Eleanor Rathbone however voted against it because it did not go far enough (Hansard, 9 March 1933). The issue was raised again in 1945 by Barbara Ayrton Gould, a newly elected Labour MP, and she was told that there could be no unilateral action within the Commonwealth (Hansard, 15 November 1945). Indeed, only when this problem was finally resolved in 1948 was the government prepared to act on what had been a long-standing feminist grievance. Government legislation in that year at last gave married women their own independent citizenship. The right of a woman to give British citizenship to her husband in the way that a man can confer it on his wife has not been fully granted, however, in the attempt to reduce male immigration (Atkins and Hoggett, 1984; Carter, 1988).

Another long-standing campaign within the House which had wide-spread support from women MPs of both parties was the fight against the marriage bar. This particular struggle had its origin in an amendment moved by Major Hills (Conservative) to the government's Sex Disqualification (Removal) Bill in 1919. This measure was designed to remove disqualification on the ground of sex 'from the exercise of any public function, civil or judicial office, any civil profession or vocation or incorporated society or juror service'. Major Hills's amendment added the word marriage to the bill as well as sex with the objective, as he stated plainly, of preventing the operation of the marriage bar in the civil service. The government accepted the amendment, for reasons that are not altogether clear, but explicitly rejected its applicability to the civil service, which was to retain its marriage bar that the government believed to be essential. It accepted the possibility of exceptions to the rule, but in practice these were rare and even by 1937 only eight exceptions had been made (Zimmeck, 1984). Hills's amendment, therefore, although accepted by both the House of Commons and the government, was immediately made ineffective in so far as the civil service was concerned. The teaching profession was not however specifically excluded from the provisions of the Act and when, during the 1920s, a marriage bar was increasingly imposed on women teachers, the impulse of those who opposed it was to turn to the provisions of the Sex Disqualification (Removal) Act which, because of this amendment, appeared to make such a bar illegal.

In 1925 the issue was raised in the House of Commons by Nancy Astor but Lord Percy made it clear in his reply that the government did not intend to intervene (Hansard, 26 November 1925). Moreover, several attempts to raise the issue in the law courts made it abundantly clear that, so far as the marriage bar was concerned, the Act was not deemed to be applicable. Faced with what seemed to be a deadlock NUSEC sponsored a new bill which was intended specifically to give married women the right to work. Major Hills, the sponsor of the original amendment in 1919, referred to the ingenuity of the courts which had found a way around the intentions of the Act, but the Financial Secretary to the Treasury spoke approvingly of marriage bars because they discouraged the employment of women. He also reiterated the argument of the courts that the 1919 Act simply rendered the appointment of a married woman valid. It did not confer any obligation to employ married women on either the government or the local education authorities, an interpretation of course quite contrary to the original intentions of the Act. Women MPs who spoke in support of the bill included not only the feminist, Nancy Astor, but two Labour MPs, Margaret Bondfield and Susan Lawrence, who rarely spoke out on feminist issues. Nevertheless in spite of support from many male MPs the voting 63 to 84 meant defeat (Hansard, 29 April 1927).

The fight against the marriage bar was still, as we have seen, an important part of the feminist agenda but after 1927 it was not an important issue within Parliament itself, although it was not forgotten. In 1939, for example, Edith Summerskill raised the issue of the marriage bar in the police (Hansard, 9 March 1939). During the war the marriage bar was put into temporary abeyance in both the civil service and in teaching, but efforts were maintained during the war to ensure that it was not allowed to return. Thelma Cazalet-Keir, the Conservative MP who led the battle for equal pay and had been involved in the fight for equal compensation, also led the drive to end the marriage bar in the civil service. Although the bar was finally abolished in 1946 it is clear that the cabinet was motivated less by considerations of equality for married women than by the postwar labour shortage (Smith, 1984a).

Similar considerations applied to the marriage bar in teaching, which was abolished in 1944 as a result of an amendment to the Education Act of that year. This was moved by Hamilton Kerr, a Conservative MP, and was eventually accepted by the government although initially there had been pressure from the Board of Education to oppose it. The Board's Parliamentary Secretary, James Chuter Ede, took the opposite view although, as he pointed out, not for what he called 'negative and feminist' grounds, but to restrict the influence of 'sex-starved spinsters' in teaching. The prospect of a severe shortage of teachers after the war was also a consideration and Butler, who had opposed Cazalet-Keir's amendment on equal pay, agreed to the abolition of the marriage bar (Smith, 1984a).

If, however, women MPs did not make an issue of the marriage bar during the 1930s, there was nevertheless serious concern among them on the unfair treatment of married women in matters concerning insurance for both unemployment and sickness. The concern expressed was mainly from Labour MPs, some of whom felt strongly enough to oppose their own government on the issue. Although Ellen Wilkinson had protested, as early as 1926, that married women were being refused unemployment benefit, it was the Anomalies Act of 1931 which caused the greatest concern. A clause was introduced into unemployment insurance in 1921, requiring all applicants to prove they were

genuinely seeking work. This clause was removed by the Labour government in 1930 but reintroduced by them in 1931, with the object of
eliminating fraudulent claims from women who did not intend to return to work after marriage. There had been a rise in the number of
married women claimants between 1927 and 1930 as a result of the
rise in unemployment, especially in textiles, and although the declared
intention of the Anomalies Act was to combat fraud, Eleanor Rathbone
(Independent) protested that married women were being 'disqualified
in shoals' (Hansard, 27 November 1931). The minister, Margaret
Bondfield, defended the Act but Marion Phillips, a Labour MP and at
that time secretary of the SJC, while agreeing that abuse should be
stopped, warned that the SJC was totally against any attempt to sweep
married women out of unemployment insurance (Hansard, 8 July 1931).
Ellen Wilkinson was also involved in the protest as were two other
Labour MPs, Jennie Lee and Cynthia Mosely (Hansard, 15 July 1931).

There were further protests in 1932 during the discussions on the
Health Insurance and Contributions Bill. This reduced sickness benefits for all women on the ground of their higher sickness rates, but
married women in particular were attacked in an amendment which
would have required women to requalify as new entrants on marriage.
The amendment was defeated largely because of the opposition of the
women MPs in alliance with the Labour Party (Gilbert, 1970). At this
time, because of the landslide against Labour in 1931, all but two of
the women in the House were Conservatives, so that their vote with
Labour against the amendment was a protest against their own party
(Harrison, 1986).

In spite of these protests there was surprisingly little opposition to
the unfavourable treatment accorded to married women in the Beveridge
Report in 1942 and the subsequent legislation (Carter, 1988). Some
limited protest came from two Labour women, Barbara Castle and
Leah Manning in 1946 (Hansard, 22 May 1946), but it was some time
before any consistent feminist opposition emerged. In 1954, however,
both Edith Summerskill and Jean Mann drew attention to the extent of
discrimination against married women in national insurance (Hansard,
14 December 1954). Yet it was not until 1974 that Barbara Castle's
Social Security Act introduced proposals which moved away from the
Beveridge doctrine of female dependency, although even then with
only limited success (Land, 1985).

One reason for the widespread acceptance of the Beveridge Report
during and after the war was the strength of 'new' feminism within

feminism itself during these years. Feminists, as we saw in an earlier chapter, accepted that married women had a primarily domestic role and believed that the main task of feminism was to improve the conditions of wives and mothers at home. This may also explain the lack of interest at the end of the war in the provision of nurseries for working mothers. Only Barbara Castle in Parliament seems to have argued for their retention and even outspoken feminists like Leah Manning believed that mothers with young children should not go out to work (Hansard, 12 June 1947).

Nevertheless, if the focus at this time was on the home rather than on the workplace, so far as married women were concerned there was, as we have seen, considerable dissatisfaction with the financial situation of the economically dependent housewife, especially if, as was increasingly the case during these years, there was a breakdown in the marriage, leading to divorce or separation. In the House of Commons and later in the House of Lords Edith Summerskill took the lead in the fight to secure some measure of economic independence for house- wives even if they had no earnings of their own, and most of the successful legislation on this issue was the result of her efforts.

The campaign really began during the war when she raised the issue of a wife's savings out of the housekeeping, which a recent case had established legally belonged to the husband and not the wife (Hansard, 16 July 1943). However, the first attempt at a bill to allow a divorced or deserted wife some rights to the matrimonial home, including the transfer of tenancy, was not made by Summerskill herself but by a Conservative woman MP, Evelyn Hill. At this time Summerskill was herself a member of the government and did not take part in the debate but Evelyn Hill got some support from women MPs of both parties though her bill was rejected by a largely unsympathetic House of Commons (Hansard, 26 January 1951). A year later, with Labour out of office, Summerskill introduced her own bill. This, entitled a Wom- en's Disabilities Bill, empowered employers to pay maintenance out of wages on behalf of defaulters, a measure which feminists had been urging since the 1920s. It also secured for the wife certain furniture and household effects and, in certain cases, tenancy. A third clause gave a wife the legal right to an adequate allowance. This bill too was unsuccessful (Hansard, 25 April 1952).

In 1957 Joan Vickers (Conservative) introduced another bill which provided for the payment of arrears of maintenance out of earnings and this bill successfully passed its second reading (Hansard, 1 March

1957). Although introduced by a Conservative MP, it was supported by three Labour women MPs, Eirene White, Edith Summerskill and Lena Jeger. Later in the year Butler introduced a government bill, arguing that it had been made necessary by the increased number of divorces and the cost to the National Assistance Board. In spite of fierce opposition from lawyers the bill was finally approved in March 1958 (Hansard, 25 March 1958). In 1963 the divorced or deserted wife won further rights when Edith Summerskill, now a Life Peeress, piloted her Married Women' Property Bill through the Lords. This gave deserted wives the right both to their savings and to the occupancy of the family home. After passage through the House of Commons it became law in 1964 (Smart, 1984).

The changes in the divorce laws in 1969 introduced for the first time the concept of irretrievable marriage breakdown as a ground for divorce with no assumptions about the conduct of either party. This made it easier for either or both parties to a broken marriage to marry again. The financial position of the first wife, who could now be divorced without her consent, was hence left in jeopardy and the government had to face a great deal of pressure to amend the law with respect to family property. Following the successful passage of the divorce legislation the government introduced the Matrimonial Proceedings and Property Act which went some way forward in recognizing the economic value of a wife's services within marriage (Smart, 1984). Under this new law, for example, the ownership of property acquired during marriage must be attributed to the spouses jointly (Stetson, 1982).

There were several other issues which were of particular concern to women in the House. Although the number of women MPs was still very small, the early 1920s saw concerted action to extend the suffrage to women on the same terms as men. The Act of 1918 had limited the vote not only to women over 30, but also to women who were either the wives of local government electors or local government electors themselves. This meant that young women were disfranchised as well as domestic servants, women living in furnished rooms, all of whom did not qualify to vote in local government elections. A number of attempts were made to extend the franchise to all women over the age of 21, although it was ten years before Stanley Baldwin, a Conservative Prime Minister, introduced a new women's suffrage bill in 1928. This reform was supported by women from all parties with the single exception of the Duchess of Atholl who doubted whether women really wanted it (Hansard, 29 February 1924). Nancy Astor was its strongest supporter and indeed on one occasion voted with the opposition and against her own party (Hansard, 20 February 1925).

There was also collaboration between women MPs when the extension of women's suffrage in India was debated in Parliament. At this time there were no Labour women in the House but Eleanor Rathbone, an Independent, was supported by several women Conservatives, including not only the feminists, Nancy Astor, Irene Ward and Mavis Tate, but even non-feminists like the Duchess of Atholl and Florence Horsbrugh. The Liberal MP, Megan Lloyd George, joined their campaign and in consequence the government made several concessions which improved the voting rights of Indian women (Hansard, 11 December 1934, 7 May 1935, 10 May 1935).

The issue of women police was, as we have seen, taken up by a variety of women's groups and, although it never involved more than a small number of women in the House, they were drawn from different party backgrounds. Both Nancy Astor (Conservative) and Margaret Wintringham (Liberal) gave it considerable attention at a time when they were the only two women in the House. Later two Labour MPs, Ellen Wilkinson and Edith Picton Tubervill, were prominent in the campaign (Carrier, 1988). The concern to extend the number of policewomen was linked specifically with the need to protect women and especially children from sexual abuse. This was a matter of great concern for Nancy Astor who was disturbed, like many feminists, at the inadequate punishments meted out by magistrates for assaults on children. Indeed the leniency with which sexual assaults were treated in the courts led to pressure not only for more women police but more women magistrates (Hansard, 12 July 1923).

Concern with the sexual abuse of women and children was also behind questions from women in Parliament on the treatment of women in British territories overseas. In 1929, for example the Duchess of Atholl raised the issue of female circumcision (Hansard, 11 December 1929), and the following year Nancy Astor drew attention to the system of 'mui tsai' in both Hong Kong and Malaysia (Hansard, 29 January 1930). This was a system which allowed the sale of little girls, sometimes as servants who were seriously overworked, but sometimes to brothels. During the 1930s anxiety was expressed by a number of women MPs. They included Susan Lawrence and Edith Picton Tubervill, both from the Labour Party, and the Conservative, Florence Horsbrugh.

Eleanor Rathbone was also involved in a number of issues concerning the sexual abuse of children in British territories.

Protest against the double standard of sexual morality was an important element in nineteenth century feminism and was indeed a very live issue in the years up to and including the first world war. There was also considerable feminist support for the attempt to raise the age of consent for indecent assault to 16, which culminated in the Criminal Law Amendment Act of 1922 (Jeffreys, 1985). This was supported in the House by Margaret Wintringham (Hansard, 5 July 1922). In 1925 Nancy Astor, an enthusiastic supporter of the Association for Moral and Social Hygiene, introduced a bill designed to reform the law on prostitution and street soliciting which was a particularly blatant example of the double standard. Prostitution itself was not an offence, so the client escaped unscathed, but every year about three hundred women were arrested on charges of solicitation or annoyance. Moreover they were presumed guilty on the basis of a statement by a single police officer (Pugh, 1992, p. 248). Astor's bill did not however go beyond its first reading (Hansard, 22 June 1926).

Perhaps surprisingly, it was 1950 before the law on prostitution was successfully challenged. In that year Barbara Castle moved an amendment to the Criminal Law Amendment Bill, then under discussion, in order to extend the protection of the law to prostitutes. This amendment was unanimously approved by the House and made it possible to bring, for example, traffic in prostitutes within the scope of the law (Hansard, 13 December 1950). In 1956 there was a further change when the Sexual Offences Act of that year made it an offence for a man persistently to solicit, thus bringing a measure of equality into the situation. In 1959, however, the Street Offences Act not only did nothing further to equalize the situation between men and women but in some ways made the situation of the prostitute worse than it had been before, since it facilitated the organization of prostitution in male hands (Wilson, 1977).

The purpose of the Act, indeed, was in no way to improve the position of prostitutes, but simply to clear them from the streets. Nor was it in any way an attack on the double standard, since it was to be the prostitute who was harassed by the provisions of the Act, and not her client. Several women MPs took the opportunity during the debate to criticize the new legislation on these grounds. Lena Jeger (Labour) for example pointed out that the bill, which still used the old derogatory terminology of 'common prostitute', abolished the need to prove annoyance and gave excessive power to the police. She was supported in the debate by another Labour MP, Eirene White, and others who voted against the bill included Labour MPs Jennie Lee, Barbara Castle and Edith Summerskill. Women in the Conservative Party supported the bill with the exception of Joan Vickers, but so did several Labour Members, including Freda Corbet and Jean Mann. It was not therefore a straightforward party issue. On the other hand, it was not seen by most women as a gender issue either, and if for some it was an argument about the double standard, these women were in a minority. Moreover, although there was support from some of the men in the House, the bill was a popular one and passed its third reading with ease, with 131 in favour and only 28 against (Hansard, 29 January 1959, 22 April 1959). It is just possible however that if the debate had taken place ten years later it might have had a different outcome.

In the years following the second world war most feminist groups, as we have seen, were in decline and feminism itself appears in some respects to have lost its way. This decline is reflected in the House of Commons where, with the exception of the campaigns for equal pay, there was little pressure from women in the House on issues that might be described as feminist. Even the issue of the economically dependent housewife did not involve women MPs to the extent of earlier campaigns, both before and during the war. Moreover, in the debate on the Street Offences Bill in 1959 only a small number of women MPs took a feminist line. Nevertheless there were a few occasions when women MPs formed an alliance of protest on issues which concerned them as women. In 1945, for example, the government's proposal to pay family allowances to fathers provoked considerable opposition, not only from women's groups outside Parliament but from women in the House, led by Eleanor Rathbone herself, and the proposal was defeated (Land, 1975).

In 1949 a Conservative MP, Peter Thorneycroft, introduced a motion on the provision of analgesia in childbirth, which gained the support of many women MPs who used their own experiences to good effect in the House. Leah Manning, a Labour MP, seconded the motion, arguing that it should not be a party matter and asked members of the Labour Party to vote for it. As many as five Labour women did so in spite of opposition from the government. The bill was defeated at the third reading but there was sufficient support in the House to force Bevan, then Minister of Health, to give assurances that everything would be done to ensure that analgesia was available to women who wanted it (Hansard, 4 March 1949, 15 March 1949, 8 July 1949).

These however are isolated incidences and Vallance has argued that it was the issue of abortion which in 1974 produced a level of unity amongst women in the House which was quite unprecedented (Vallance, 1979). The immediate impetus was an unsuccessful attempt by James White to limit the working of the 1967 Abortion Act. In the voting on his amendment only two women supported him and eleven were in opposition (Hansard, 7 February 1974, 26 February 1974). The debate itself, moreover, makes it clear that it was seen not only as a feminist issue but one of special concern to women. Indeed Lena Jeger, protesting at the composition of the Select Committee on Abortion which had just been appointed, argued that such a Committee should consist primarily of women MPs. (Hansard, 26 February 1975)

In trying to understand the views expressed and the exceptional coherence of women in the House at this time it is necessary to recognize the effect of the new women's movement, which was not only already highly influential but placed a very special significance on abortion as a woman's right. Previously women MPs had not, on the whole, made an issue of abortion, nor indeed of contraception. Indeed when, in 1926, Ernest Thurtle introduced a bill to authorize local authorities to incur expenditure on birth control information at their welfare centres, he was supported by only one of the four women then in the House (Hansard, 9 May 1926). It was not until much later that Nancy Astor became so convinced of the necessity to provide such information that both she and Mavis Tate spoke out in favour of birth control as a way of reducing the high level of illegal abortions (Hansard, 17 July 1935).

As with birth control so the first attempt to raise abortion law reform in the House was by a man, Joseph Reeves, a Labour and Co-operative MP, whose motion was talked out after only one minute of debate (Potts, Diggory and Peel, 1977). Although questions on abortion were raised by Lena Jeger in 1957 and 1958 (Hansard, 20 December 1957, 20 February 1958), the next attempt to change the law was also by a man, Kenneth Robinson, also representing the Labour Party. His bill was talked out after a brief debate in which no woman spoke, and there was no vote (Hansard, 10 February 1961). Only in 1965 was the abortion issue presented by a woman, when Renee Short, a newly elected Labour MP moved another bill with the support, as she claimed, of a large number of women's organizations. Even at this stage, however, of the nine MPs who argued in support of her bill seven were men and only two were women (Hansard, 15 June 1965).

Although Renee Short's bill was also talked out, attitudes were already changing, influenced in part at least by the thalidomide tragedy in 1961 which had made Edith Summerskill, now in the House of Lords, an outspoken advocate of a change in the law. By 1964, moreover, a new leadership had revitalized the Abortion Law Reform Association. At this time however the ALRA was by no means a woman's organization. Not only were a third of the members male but also one half of the executive (Hindell and Simms, 1971). Nevertheless it was able to secure the support of many women's groups.

The year 1966 saw the successful attempt by the Liberal, David Steel, to introduce a bill to reform the law by extending the legal grounds for an abortion to include social as well as medical considerations. The bill itself was helped by the decision of the Labour government to allow a free vote. The second reading was passed by a large majority and only three women opposed it, the Conservatives Jill Knight and Alice Cullen, and Shirley Williams from the Labour side (Hansard, 22 July 1966). The third reading also saw only three women in opposition, Jill Knight, Shirley Williams and Irene Ward, and ten women in support (Hansard, 13 July 1967). Although the bill received support from both men and women a slightly higher proportion of women voted in its favour.

It is clear that during the 1960s, and especially by the end of the decade, the mood of the women in the House of Commons was changing. In 1970 Joyce Butler, a Labour and Co-operative MP, introduced a bill to outlaw discrimination against women, the first bill of this kind since 1919. Her bill was supported by a group of nine women, mostly from the Labour Party but including two Conservatives and one Scottish Nationalist. It passed its second reading without a vote but went no further (Hansard, 9 February 1970). The year 1972, with the Conservative Party now in power, saw another bill, this time introduced by the Labour MP William Hamilton, but it was talked out by what was later described as a 'minority of neolithic Tory male Members' (Hansard, 3 February 1973). There was strong support from most of the women present and only one, the Conservative Patricia Hornby Smith, opposed it on the ground that it was not practicable. The Minister of State for the Home Office was also opposed to it on the grounds that there was little discrimination in employment and that it was justified on biological grounds (Hansard, 28 January 1972).

The next move came from Baroness Seear in the House of Lords. Despite government opposition her bill passed its second reading with a substantial majority. Subsequently a select committee revealed the existence of considerable discrimination. By this time the government was prepared to withdraw its opposition but a change of government meant that it was the Labour Party which was responsible for the Anti-Discrimination Act of 1975. The intention of the Act was to end discrimination on the grounds of both sex and marriage. It was to apply to employment, housing, the provision of goods and services, and related advertising. Protective legislation was however to be excluded and so was the issue of women's ordination (Hansard, 23 July 1974). In the debate on the bill some doubt was expressed by women Members on the introduction of male midwives, as well as on the abolition of single-sex trade unions, but Joan Lester argued strongly that if women were allowed to exclude men, they could hardly forbid men to exclude women. Maureen Colquhoun, in a strongly feminist speech, put the case for some form of positive discrimination, but this was not generally accepted.

It would seem, therefore, that even if women MPs on the whole gave priority to their party, a number of gender issues were seen by them as important enough to campaign for with energy and determination, and even at times to make them challenge their own party. There were considerable differences between individual MPs and, clearly, gender issues mattered very much more to some than to others. Moreover, if by no means all the women were feminists, very few could be described as anti-feminist, and even those who were, like the Duchess of Atholl, found themselves more than once allied with outright feminists like Nancy Astor and Eleanor Rathbone.

Nor do gender issues seem on the whole to have divided the women MPs along party lines. Certainly there were party differences between them, which were felt very strongly, but they rarely took the form of disagreement about matters of gender. Although they accepted the discipline of the party, and this limited the extent of their collaboration across party lines, such collaboration did occur from time to time on issues which they saw as particularly important to them as women. Moreover those women who can be described as active feminists were not confined to any single party.

Many women MPs also maintained ties of one kind or another with one or more women's organizations. Nancy Astor, for example, mixed freely with the leaders of NUSEC although she was not herself a member, and Ray Strachey acted as her secretary for many years and provided her with a great deal of information which she used in her speeches in the House. Margaret Wintringham also worked closely with NUSEC during the short time she was in the House. Eleanor Rathbone was its president for many years. Nancy Astor also had a long and close relationship with the Association for Moral and Social Hygiene (Alberti, 1989). Leah Manning, one of the most active feminists in the House between 1945 and 1950, was a member of the Women's Freedom League, which also helped Ellen Wilkinson get into Parliament (Brookes, 1967). Mavis Tate, active between 1935 and 1945, was also active in the League and was for a time its president. Edith Summerskill, who entered Parliament in 1938, was president for many years of the Married Women's Association. A number of women MPs also had ties with women's groups within the labour and trade union movement.

It is clear therefore that through this kind of tie the views of women's organizations were brought before the House of Commons, not only through political lobbying in general, but through a close association with a particular woman Member. Moreover, even without such specific ties women MPs may have felt a particular concern with women's groups simply because of their identification with them as women. Irene Ward, for example, told the House in 1959 that it was her policy to work closely with women's organizations. Consequently, although women in the House never worked together as a women's group in any formal way, it would be a mistake to dismiss altogether the existence for many of them of a sense of gender identity which cut across the differences of party, which otherwise divided them.

By the late 1960s these ties seemed to have become more widespread, especially on the Labour side of the House. In 1967 the National Executive Committee set up a working group to explore discrimination against women, and Betty Lockwood, the Chief Woman's Officer between 1967 and 1975, was active in promoting equal rights within the labour movement (Carter, 1988). This change of emphasis was reflected in the House of Commons and by the early 1970s there was new militancy amongst Labour women. Indeed, Vallance has argued that the change of emphasis by 1974 was enormous (Vallance, 1979).

In evaluating the performance of women MPs and especially their achievements for women a great deal has been made of their refusal to see themselves in any real sense as representatives of women. It has been argued in this chapter that this was only partly true. A much more potent factor was party loyalty which inhibited women from challenging their own party. More important still, however, was the fact that during the greater part of the period of this study neither the Labour nor the Conservative leadership was sympathetic to the goals of the women's movement. Consequently, whatever party they belonged to, or whatever party was in power, for most of the time women MPs, campaigning on issues of gender, were forced to fight against what was in most cases a hostile government, even when it was a government controlled by their own party. It must also be remembered that the number of women in Parliament was always very small. This was particularly true of the period before the second world war, when at its highest it represented only 2.4 per cent of the total number of MPs. The situation after the war improved and in 1964 there were as many as 28 women, 4.4 per cent of the total (Pugh, 1992, p. 159). Clearly, however, even at 4.4 per cent their power to influence events was ridiculously small, no matter how united they may have been.

For this reason Part II of this study will turn away from the women's movement and look instead at the context in which it had of necessity to operate. For the purpose of analysis three aspects of this context have been differentiated, the ideological, the political, and the economic, although in practice these different aspects tended to operate together, sometimes reinforcing each other, but at times pulling in different directions. In general it was a context hostile to the aims and ambitions of feminism but this was not always so and it will be the purpose of Part II to explore the changing context in some detail, and to examine some of the ways in which it influenced the development of feminism and the women's movement.

PART II
The Background to the Feminist Struggle

5. The Ideological Context

When in 1918 the vote was at least partially achieved for women and when shortly afterwards they were allowed to sit in Parliament, those who had worked for women's suffrage believed that they had won a significant victory. This belief must have been strengthened by the election manifestos in the 1918 general election, since the successful Conservative/Liberal government had promised to remove all existing inequalities of the law as between men and women. The Labour Party manifesto too had claimed not only that it stood for equal rights for both sexes, but that the 'Labour Party *is* the women's Party' (Craig, 1970). Moreover, during the next few years several measures were accepted by Parliament which seemed to suggest that these pledges had to be taken seriously. In 1919, for example, the Sex Discrimination (Removal) Act appeared at the time to promise an end to discrimination against women on the grounds of both sex and marriage. In 1922 the Criminal Law Amendment Act made changes in the age of consent which had long been sought for by many in the women's movement and in 1923 the grounds of divorce were at long last made equal for men and women

Writing much later, in 1936, Ray Strachey also drew attention to the 1922 Law of Property Act which improved the position of women whose husbands died intestate, the 1925 Summary Jurisdiction (Separation and Maintenance) Act, which allowed a woman to be granted a separation order before she had left her husband, and in 1925 the Guardianship of Infants Act which, even if it did not make men and women equal, at least redressed a number of particular grievances (Strachey, 1936). Other measures during the 1920s for which women's groups had worked included widows' pensions, legislation to protect unmarried mothers and, in 1929, an Act to raise the minimum age at which girls could be married from 12 to 16. Yet, as the preceding chapter has shown, many of the campaigns fought by the women's movement succeeded only after a long, hard struggle and the impetus achieved during the early 1920s was not only not maintained but was not repeated until the end of the 1960s

Even during the 1920s the women's movement and women in Parliament were forced to accept compromises, as in the case of the 1925 Guardianship of Infants Act, which gave mothers an extension of their rights but not the equality that had been asked for in the original bill (Brophy, 1982). The Sex Discrimination (Removal) Bill of 1919 was crippled from the start by the exclusion of the civil service from its provisions. Nor was it possible to use it either against the marriage bar or to allow peeresses to sit in the House of Lords. Indeed, in practice it did little more than open the legal profession to women, and to allow them to become magistrates and, within certain limitations, to sit on juries.

The consistent and indeed persistent opposition faced by women's organizations indicates an active hostility to feminist goals as a significant factor in British political and intellectual life even after women's right to citizenship had been granted. Indeed, as Pugh has pointed out, it was quite possible for men to accept votes for women without abandoning their traditional beliefs about the role of the two sexes (Pugh, 1992), and these beliefs continued to permeate most thinking about women long after they achieved the vote and even, as earlier chapters have shown, penetrated feminism itself.

It has sometimes been suggested that gratitude for women's services during the first world war and a new appraisal of the capabilities this revealed led to a change in attitude to women and their position in society. There is evidence however that far from having a favourable effect, the war years actually produced an accentuation of anti-feminist feeling which was intensified in the postwar period. Perrott, for example, has argued that the effect of the war, far from liberating women, contributed to putting them back in their place by a reaffirmation of traditional values. The moral threat posed by the war strengthened both the image of woman as a mother and beliefs in an essential femininity and masculinity (Perrott, 1987). Smith has made the same point, arguing that alarm over perceived wartime changes in sex roles did much to strengthen those forces seeking to restore traditional sex roles (Smith, 1990).

Although these feelings were held in check during the war by the urgent need for women to step out of their customary roles, it was made clear even at the time that this relaxation of customary roles was of a strictly temporary nature. In the trade union world, for example, permission for women to enter men's jobs was granted only on the promise by the government that any departure from prewar practice should be for the period of the war only, and in 1919 the Restoration of Pre-War Practices Act legally restored the prewar position (Hansard, 2 June 1919).

In the years immediately after the war there was a powerful reaction against the gains that women had made during the war. Anxiety centred on the issue of women's work which was pictured as depriving men of their rightful jobs, and although focused initially on the needs of ex-servicemen, it was interpreted much more widely to involve any extension of women into what had formerly been a male preserve (Mellman, 1988; Zimmeck, 1984; Kent, 1988). It has also been suggested that the dreadful experiences suffered by men at the front led to a resentment against women who had not only remained in comfort at home while men had fought and died, but had actually gained as a result of the war (Gilbert, 1987). The postwar years therefore saw a powerful reaction against women's achievements which expressed itself in attacks on the women's movement itself, even from those who had formerly been in sympathy with the movement for women's suffrage

By the 1920s, for example, D.H. Lawrence adopted a quite explicit anti-feminism, based on his belief that women were now dominant in society. Whereas earlier he had urged women to enter politics in order to express their own particular point of view, he now began to fear that their influence would be harmful to both men and women. The basis for his anti-feminism was his belief in an innate and indeed necessary difference between them which was now becoming blurred with disastrous consequences for the future. He saw men as naturally creatures of active energy and authority and this expressed itself both sexually and in an aptitude for politics which women did not share. Women, on the other hand, were emotional, intuitive and sympathetic, qualities which rendered them unfit for the world of politics. Women's sexuality too should be passive, and for this reason he condemned the clitoral orgasm which he perceived as aggressive and dominating. He came therefore to oppose not only women's entry into politics but any feminist claim which involved women stepping out of their own sphere. Even his advocacy of a greater sexual freedom for women was, therefore, severely constrained by his view of them as essentially passive partners in the sexual act (Simpson, 1982).

Lawrence's beliefs were echoed by other anti-feminists during the 1920s (Jeffreys, 1985). *Lysistrata*, for example, published in 1924, also took as its starting place a number of innate differences between men and women which made women's subordination natural and therefore right. The author, A.M. Ludovici, saw feminism as a direct consequence of man's loss of faith in his own masculinity, a process which had allowed women to move out of their distinctly subordinate role. Consequently, woman must be put back into her place if the natural order was to be restored, and must regain her lost joy in looking up to her man. For Ludovici there was a natural hostility between men and women which was restrained only by a sexual relationship between them. The leaders of the women's movement were, he believed, either spinsters or unhappily married women who, denied a satisfactory sexual relationship themselves, wanted to deny men what he called their vigorous sexuality and who hated not only men but sexuality itself (Ludovici, 1924).

Anti-feminism was not however confined to men. Arabella Keneally, writing in 1920, also saw feminism as unnatural, because it attempted to eliminate essential and indeed beneficial differences between men and women. She saw women as nearer to nature, more irresponsible, less specialized and less complex than men, who were the natural leaders. Men should therefore have the controlling voice in politics and civic affairs, although Keneally, unlike some anti-feminists, did not try to eliminate women from politics altogether. Nor in her view did women lack qualities beneficial to society but these were locked up in their role as mothers, a role so important that women could not be given unrestrained liberty of action, and young women and mothers should be protected from all employment, whether industrial or professional. Feminism was harmful because it tried to eliminate women's special qualities, seeking after neuter standards and models, and so contradicting biological laws. Moreover it destroyed not only femininity but masculinity too, producing neurotic and emasculated men and boys (Keneally, 1920).

Apart from direct attacks of this kind, which might not have mattered in themselves, feminism was undermined in more serious ways by the developing 'science' of sexology. Lawrence, Ludovici, Keneally and others like them all attacked the feminists openly but the early sexologists were sympathetic and encouraging to many feminist aims. Edward Carpenter, for example, who may along with Havelock Ellis be described as one of sexology's pioneers, was certainly not antagonistic to the suffrage movement of his day but, like the anti-feminists, he believed firmly that masculinity and femininity are fixed character-istics with their origins in biology. He also shared with Ludovici the view that feminists were women without strong sexual or maternal instincts (Rowbotham and Weeks, 1977).

Havelock Ellis, too, was ambiguous in his attitude to feminism. He believed, like Carpenter, that behaviour was fundamentally an expres-sion of biological drives, not a result of social processes. Consequently there were differences between men and women which were entirely natural and which arose in part from differences in their sexual re-sponse, and partly from women's role as mothers. Like Lawrence, he saw the male as sexually active, his role that of capture and arousal while the woman, her sexuality essentially passive, waited to be aroused. Differentiation did not however end with the sexual experience. Wom-an's task was to breed and to tend, a role bound up with the future of the race. In contrast, man was the provider. Ellis was therefore strongly critical of a number of aspects of feminism. Believing that women could not compete satisfactorily with men and should not even try, he opposed attempts to achieve equal opportunities in employment. In-stead women should fulfil their role as mothers which was important, not only for the satisfaction of their own needs but for the race (Rowbotham and Weeks, 1977).

During the 1920s these ideas became the basis of a sex therapy which defined female sexuality as passive and responsive and the male as dominating and predatory. Indeed any resistance to male domina-tion was seen as harmful to women's own sexual response which depended on their total surrender. At the same time, women's right to sexual pleasure was turned into a duty as theories of the dangers of sexual repression gained ground. There was no room within these theories to try to limit some aspects of male sexual behaviour since this was now seen as natural if not indeed uncontrollable. Those femi-nists of an earlier generation who had emphasized the harmful effects of male sexuality on women were now characterized as damaging to men and women alike. Moreover as sexual responsiveness came to be seen as desirable in a woman and frigidity on her part a cause for blame, the spinster came under attack (Jeffreys, 1985).

The distrust of the spinster, based on a view of her as someone who had repressed her natural instincts, was associated not only with her denial of her sexual needs but also with her failure to fulfil her destiny as a mother. Married women who refused to become mothers were particular objects of blame since by deliberately setting aside their duty they were harming not only their own physiological and psychological development but also the future of the race (Haldane, 1927).

This attitude was reflected at a more popular level in the world of women's magazines. The assumption that the purpose of a woman's life was the acquiring and keeping of a husband was commonplace, and the woman who had chosen a career rather than marriage was depicted as lonely and neurotic. Because keeping a husband was so important, wives were encouraged to accept a subordinate role and even an unfaithful husband was better than no husband at all (Pugh, 1992). Women were encouraged not only to marry but also to have children, and childlessness on the part of a married woman was castigated as selfish. Moreover a career was always presented as an alternative to marriage (White, 1970).

This powerful ideology which emphasized a natural biological differentiation between men and women, in which women's primary function was to serve as wives and mothers, was not restricted therefore to the enemies of feminism but was widely accepted by women as well as men. Indeed it had its parallel, as we have seen, within feminism itself (Kent, 1988). The development of the so-called 'new' feminism reflected this view very clearly, emphasizing as it did that women's primary role was as wife and mother. Feminists like Eleanor Rathbone and Dora Russell are examples of women who tried to reinterpret feminism in ways which would allow the needs of wives and mothers to occupy a more significant place. In the process Dora Russell, at least, came to accept many of the arguments of sexologists like Havelock Ellis for a differentiation between men and women which was essentially biological in nature. Unlike Ellis she used the concept of biological difference to attack male domination rather than to reinforce it, but her feminism, unlike equal rights feminism, was biological in its origin (Russell, 1973). She believed that women, because of their child-bearing role, were nearer than men to nature and to the organic world, which meant that they possessed an instinctive wisdom which men must learn to attend to (Russell, 1977).

Not all feminists followed Rathbone into the 'new' feminism and one of its most outspoken critics was the novelist, Winifred Holtby. She argued that the 'new' feminists were too sanguine in their belief that many, if not most equal rights had already been achieved, and that a great deal of injustice still existed which needed to be remedied. Nor did she have any time for what she saw as a grossly exaggerated emphasis on marriage and maternity which she believed to be no more than an excuse for the maintenance of women's political and economic disabilities (Berry and Bishop, 1985). She even went so far as to claim that women were being hounded into marriage and maternity, and was highly critical of the view that marriage was the only way to fulfilment for a woman. She also contrasted the hostility expressed towards spinsters with the tolerance shown to bachelors. At the same time she criticized the double standard which demanded celibacy only from women. She was also opposed to those current trends which exalted instinct and emotion above reason, trends which she associated above all with the writings of D.H. Lawrence and which she saw as antagonistic towards feminism (Holtby, 1934).

Nevertheless, by the 1930s the 'new' feminism was in the ascendant and, by the end of that decade, was accentuated by a panic about population decline which extended to the feminists themselves. Eleanor Rathbone, for example, was using both pro-natalist and eugenic arguments in presenting her case for family allowances and by 1941 had persuaded a group of pro-natalist reforming Conservatives to give her campaign their support (Macnicol, 1980). By this time, indeed, the feminist case was almost completely overlaid by concern for the falling birthrate on the one hand and family poverty on the other. Eva Hubback, too, who in the early 1920s had been Parliamentary secretary to NUSEC and, in that post, was responsible for much of the feminist legislation which came before Parliament, had by the 1930s turned her attention away from equal rights feminism. In 1930 for example she argued that peace was the first objective of the women's movement, followed by the preservation and welfare of the racial stock. Issues of gender equality came only third and last in her list (Banks, 1986).

The outbreak of war in 1939 brought women into the labour force in large numbers but this was regarded as a temporary measure. Moreover, every effort was made to maintain prewar practices of sex differentiation wherever this was possible, as the debates on the issues of equal pay and equal compensation show clearly (Smith, 1981). Equal pay was granted in certain circumstances during the war when a woman took over a man's job, but this concession on the part of the trade union movement was made to protect the male worker and not to benefit women. Moreover, in spite of the agreements made, very few women actually achieved equal pay, since they were faced with the opposition of both employers and men on the shop floor (Summerfield, 1984).

At the same time there was no real attempt to relieve working women from the burden of domestic work. Although it was not government policy to compel those with young children to work, many did so because the allowance for dependents of service men was too low (Allen, 1983). The labour of these women was also necessary as the demands of the war on labour continued to increase. Nevertheless, the provision of nurseries was severely handicapped by the attitude of officials at the Ministry of Health who believed that mothers of young children should be at home. Faced with pressure from the Minister of Labour, Bevin, they suggested the alternative of child minders and were sufficiently powerful to make minders rather than nurseries the official policy. Consequently, even during the war itself the great bulk of domestic work remained the responsibility of the wife and mother, even when she was engaged on war work (Summerfield, 1984).

Once the war was over many of the limited concessions made to women were withdrawn, including the war-time nurseries. The wartime relaxation of the marriage bar, intended to be temporary, was not reimposed but this was a straightforward response to a labour shortage (Smith, 1984a). The general climate of opinion had changed little in spite of the war and women were still regarded primarily as mothers or potential mothers (Riley, 1987). Indeed, Smith has argued that the war may have actually reinforced traditional ideology, since women in many respects found wartime measures difficult and unpleasant rather than challenging and liberating. This was particularly true of house-wives and mothers who faced not only the absence of their husbands but all the hardships of shortages and rationing (Smith, 1986).

The emphasis on women's role as mothers was powerfully reinforced by the pro-natalist climate which dominated the war years and was still influential for several years afterwards, until the so-called 'baby boom' made it irrelevant. The effect of Bowlby's views on the young child's need for its mother was also important especially since his theories were absorbed into social work training during the 1950s (Riley, 1983). Bowlby did not, of course, originate the belief that mothers should not go out to work, as this was already widely prevalent before the war, but he did provide what seemed, at the time, a scientific justification for the belief, and his ideas gained a very wide acceptance, especially during the 1950s.

It is clear indeed that in many ways postwar thinking was character-ized by much of the anti-feminism which we have seen to be prevalent in the years after the first world war. There was still a belief in a strongly marked differentiation between the sexes which was used to attack the concept of equal rights for women. These differences for example were used to justify a quite different curriculum for girls at school, and even the new discipline of sociology accepted the tradi-tional differentiation of roles between men and women and even romanticized it in writing about the family (Wilson, 1980). Delamont, too, has provided us with a devastating critique of the sociology of science and the sociology of the professions, which presented them as essentially male fields of work (Delamont, 1989). The Marriage Guid-ance Council, which started to expand after the war, is also shown by Elizabeth Wilson to have been not only conventional in its attitude to women but anti-feminist in much of its advice. In all its counselling work masculinity and femininity were rigidly defined and female sexu-ality, as with the prewar sexologists, seen as passive and responsive. Indeed it was advocated that women should neither demand sex nor refuse their husband's demands. As in the prewar period, too, both marriage and child-bearing were seen as duties for women and there was the same dislike of the celibate spinster and the married woman who deliberately avoided bearing children (Wilson, 1980).

Precisely the same values were purveyed by the women's magazines of the period. In the 1950s for example all the popular magazines actively discouraged women from trying to combine work and mar-riage, and only the monthly journals, catering to a middle-class clien-tele, took a different line. Advertising, too, was directed at women in their role as housewives and mothers. Only during the 1960s was there a gradual acceptance of the idea that women might combine marriage and a career (White, 1970).

Within feminism itself the ideas of the 'new' feminists seem to have strengthened in the years after the war. An important victory was gained by the equal rights feminists in 1956 when equal pay was granted to women in the civil service and in teaching but no major equal rights campaign took its place. Indeed one of the most prominent campaigners for equal rights, the NUWT, was forced to close down in 1961 as young women teachers were not joining the association in sufficient numbers (Pierotti, 1963). Another equal rights group, the Women's Freedom League, also closed down in 1961 and the National Association of Women Civil Servants in 1959.

The spread of 'new' feminist ideas was greatly helped by the fears of a declining population. Both feminists and women in the labour movement, whether they shared these fears or not, used the widespread anxiety about a falling family size to press for measures to improve the lot of those who were mothers so that they might be willing to produce more children (Riley, 1983; Lewis, 1980). Eve Hubback, in 1947, accepted this position unreservedly, arguing for a strengthening of those forces which imposed on women a belief in the central importance of their child-bearing and child-rearing function. She advocated an improvement in the facilities available to mothers at home rather than greater employment opportunities which might tempt a woman to limit the size of her family (Hubback, 1947).

Although by 1952 the panic over the declining birthrate was over, the prevailing attitude even amongst feminists was primarily pro-natalist. The feminist conference papers, *A Woman's Point of View*, published in that year and discussed in Chapter 2, came down heavily in favour of the primacy of woman's domestic role. Her responsibility for the domestic side of life, it was argued, must always take precedence over a career, especially if there were children. Moreover marriage was expected to produce children and women who did not desire children were described as 'rather unnatural'. Similarly marriage was praised as the best thing in life. Consequently, although the authors of the conference report opposed discrimination against women and wanted them to become more effective in public life, they believed that this must not be allowed to interfere with women's natural destiny as wives and mothers. It was accepted that some women would want to avoid this destiny but it was made very clear that such women were in some way 'unnatural'.

A very similar set of attitudes was expressed in Judith Hubback's study of college-educated wives, published in 1957. Women who want to combine marriage and a career are warned that this must not involve any neglect of homes, husbands and children. Moreover girls contemplating a career are warned that motherhood involves a much more radical disturbance to their lives than fatherhood and that, in consequence, the expense of training for a specialized career is less justified for a girl. Although Bowlby is cited as an authority, it is clear that Bowlby's theories are of less significance than a belief in women's destiny as wives and mothers, and, indeed, in demonstration of this point the author argues that it is more natural to have more rather than fewer children (Hubback, 1957). This essentially conservative ideology remained typical of feminism throughout the 1950s, and it was only in the 1960s and 1970s that new attitudes began to emerge.

Throughout the greater part of the period of this study, therefore, the prevalent ideology, even within much of feminism itself, was one which imprisoned women in a doctrine of separate spheres, based on a theory of natural and indeed biological differences. Women were destined to be wives and mothers and for the sake of both their own psychological health and the future of the race it was important that this destiny should be fulfilled. There were no moves to force women to marry but, as we have seen, the spinster was often regarded with a measure of contempt and even hostility, which was not customarily awarded to the unmarried man. Married women, on the other hand, might well be prevented from working, even if they had no young children or no children at all. Moreover the avoidance of motherhood by the married woman was regarded as both selfish and unnatural.

This particular ideology was shared more or less equally by both the main political parties, so that any feminist claim which attempted to challenge it met with opposition and sometimes indeed with a great deal of hostility. At first sight, it is true, the Labour Party appeared to be a most promising ally because of its more radical ideology. Moreover in the years before the first world war the Labour Party had gained much feminist support for its endorsement in 1912 of women's suffrage as official party policy. Nevertheless, it quickly became apparent that many men, especially in the trade union movement, were hostile to many of the more radical aims of feminism. In the first place they believed firmly that all the problems of women workers were an aspect of their class position and not of their gender and were suspicious of any attempt to bring gender into the political discussion (Smith, 1984b). The trade union movement, in particular, saw the basic unit as the family rather than its individual members and had little sympathy for any claims for the economic independence of wives and mothers. Women at work, indeed, represented mainly the undercutting of male wages; trade union policy remained that of the maintenance of the family wage at a level which would enable a man not only to support his family but keep his wife at home (Lewis, 1986).

The Conservative Party too was traditional in its attitude to women and the family. It was prepared to welcome women into the Party and, indeed, they were better represented at national conferences than women in the labour and trade union movements, but their political role was nevertheless a subordinate one, and their significance for the Party was predominantly in their role as wives and particularly mothers. Moreover Conservative women accepted this view of themselves and did not, like Labour women, challenge the male leaders of their party on issues of gender. Indeed the habit of loyalty was not broken until the Criminal Justice Bill in 1939 proposed the abolition of flogging, a proposal which aroused fears of sexual violence against women and children. There was another period of revolt on the issue of law and order in the 1960s but, although the emphasis was still on women and children as victims, the context of the debate was the leniency of penalties rather than any specific gender issue. Not until the 1960s was there a cautious approach among Conservative women towards equality between men and women. The Conservative Party therefore was able to maintain the doctrine of separate spheres without any real challenge from the ranks of organized Conservative women (Pugh, 1988; Campbell, 1987).

There were therefore many more similarities between the parties in their ideology than might at first be supposed. The radicalism of the Labour Party did not extend to the family and like the Conservatives they were more concerned to strengthen and preserve the traditional family than to challenge its assumptions. For this reason both the main parties were only prepared to give a welcome to feminist reforms if they appeared to strengthen the family. In Parliament, opposition to feminist claims was frequently expressed in the crudest ideological terms. It was made clear, for example, that married women had no right to be in employment for, as one Labour Member phrased it in 1919, 'man must be the toiler and woman must attend to her home duties' (Hansard, 2 June 1919, p. 1771). For this reason equal pay was demanded not as a matter of justice to a woman worker but because it would lead to the withdrawal of some women from employment. The argument against equal pay, on the other hand, was also based on the role of the husband as breadwinner. Unequal pay, the Financial Secretary to the Treasury declared in 1936, was necessary because a man was a potential husband and father. Interestingly, in the same debate, Eleanor Rathbone made precisely the same point, arguing that men's salaries not only 'remunerate the work of the worker but also provide for future generations of workers' (Hansard, 7 June 1935).

The same argument was still being used after the war, this time under a Labour administration. Hugh Gaitskell, speaking as Chancellor of the Exchequer, rejected the pressure for equal pay because the majority of men had families dependent on them (Hansard, 20 June 1951), an argument repeated a few months later by Douglas Jay

(Hansard, 2 August 1951). Strictly speaking these statements were not true since only about one-third of occupied males had dependent children, but they illustrate the power of an ideology which still regarded the husband as the breadwinner.

The same kind of ideology was used to justify the marriage bar and to oppose any suggestion that married women had the right to work. As early as 1919, during the discussion of the Sex Disqualification (Removal) Bill, the Solicitor General stated categorically that married women should bear children (Hansard, 27 October 1919). Eight years later, during an unsuccessful move to make the marriage bar illegal, the Financial Secretary to the Treasury opposed the bill on the ground that it might encourage the neglect of a woman's duties in the home (Hansard, 29 April 1927).

Within the civil service such attitudes as these were especially powerful. In 1918 for example the Government Actuary opposed greater Treasury support to women workers after childbirth because this might act as an inducement to women to go out to work (Lewis, 1986). The Treasury indeed believed strongly in a gender-based structure of work in the civil service and set its face firmly against calls in the House of Commons for an equality of opportunity policy as well as equal pay and for the abolition of the marriage bar. It has been argued that the exemption of the civil service from the Sex Disqualification (Removal) Act of 1922 was the result of direct pressure on the government by the Treasury (Zimmeck, 1984).

There is evidence that behind this emphasis on women's role as wives and mothers was a fear that women might actually be failing in this important duty. Jane Lewis has pointed out that it was a common belief that infant mortality was a consequence of a failure on the part of women as mothers, and mothers who worked were seen as neglecting their duties in the home. Only well-to-do women who could afford adequate domestic help were exempt from this charge (Lewis, 1980). At the same time there was a considerable and growing anxiety that women were turning away from motherhood altogether. Roy Harrod, for example, in his evidence to the Royal Commission on Equal Pay argued that it might entice women away from what he described as their rightful work of child-bearing (Wilson, 1980).

The problem of unemployment also played its part in fuelling public resentment against the married woman at work. The beliefs that married women did not need to earn and that it was unjust for two incomes to go into one family helped to maintain support for the marriage bar for as long as unemployment was a serious problem. During and after the war, when women were needed, the marriage bar was lifted, and in 1947 a heavy demand for women in manual work led to a special government recruitment drive (Crofts, 1986). Nevertheless every effort was made to recruit women without disturbing the traditional division of labour in the home. The Labour government was aware of the need to meet the demand for female labour but it wanted to do so while promoting a family life which depended on women maintaining their traditional role as child-rearers as well as child-bearers. The pattern that eventually developed during the 1960s was one in which the husband was still the main wage-earner and in which the employment of the wife, intermittent and often part-time, did not really challenge the principle of a wife's financial dependency on a husband, laid down by Beveridge (Wilson, 1980; Lewis, 1990).

The ideology of a separation of roles therefore had a significant influence on government policy during virtually the whole of the period under study and thus placed considerable obstacles in the way of many of the goals of the women's movement. This was true in particular of those aims which related to the employment of women, whether as manual or non-manual workers, but the belief in a sexual differentiation of labour also had an influence on the relationship between men and women in the home. This involved not only the division of function in which domestic responsibility was centred on the woman, but a legal differentiation which gave greater power to the husband. From the early nineteenth century the feminist movement had attacked what was at that time a grossly unequal relationship and had indeed secured several successes, but by 1918 the position was still as unequal in many respects. The various attempts by the women's movement to secure a greater measure of equality were however only successful after a severe struggle in which opponents claimed that to grant this equality would be to threaten the unity of the family and to deny the husband his natural position as its head (Brophy, 1982).

Moreover the belief that it was natural for a wife to be subordinate to her husband was also extended to situations outside the home. In the civil service, for example, it was considered that women should in the main fill subordinate positions and appropriate that they should perform mostly routine tasks (Zimmeck, 1984). Within the teaching profession it was widely accepted that women teachers should not teach older boys. It was also regarded as highly detrimental for boys to see a woman in charge of male teachers, an attitude which seriously impeded the opportunities of women teachers in the mixed schools which were becoming increasingly common (Oram, 1987, 1989). The same belief in women's natural subordination to men also hindered women's progress in the Church of England (Heeney, 1988).

Undoubtedly, too, this belief in male superiority played its part in maintaining women in a mainly subordinate position within the labour and trade union movement and helped to foster the attitude that women's issues were not important. It also helped to maintain a view of the working-class family which overlooked the extent to which women might be exploited or even ill-used. Lambertz, for example, has argued that the full extent of unequal power relations between husbands and wives has never been fully explored. Feminists in the past have tended to emphasize the role of limited financial resources rather than that of physical violence, so that until recently battered wives did not become a particular symbol of the disabilities suffered by married women (Lambertz, 1990).

By the late 1960s what has sometimes been called the 'domestic ideology' was beginning to be challenged by the modern feminist movement which has been highly critical of the so-called 'new' feminism and its influence on the women's movement. A discussion of modern feminism has no place here although it has clearly informed the analysis upon which this study has been based. For most of the period between 1918 and 1970, however, the ideology described in this chapter dominated the political scene and was even powerful enough to influence the women's movement itself. On the other hand, ideology alone does not explain the whole of the context within which feminism operated during these years. There was an important political context, too, in which considerations of party rivalry, of appeal to the electorate, or relationships between government and party, as well as cross-party alliances all played their part. It is to these issues that we now turn.

6. The Political Context

As the previous chapter tried to show, the political parties held an ideological position which was largely unsympathetic to the women's movement and especially to those aspects of it which involved any radical reappraisal of the relationship between men and women. In spite of this some at least of the goals of feminism were achieved, either in whole or in part, during the period of this study, and in order to understand why this should have been so the present chapter will look in more detail than in previous chapters at the political context in which the political parties operated, and the political struggles in which they engaged. In particular it will examine the various pressures on parties and governments, and their effect on party policy.

Although there are a great many such pressures, it is the electorate itself which is perhaps the most important since it is from the electorate that a government derives its power. At the same time because, in any election, the responses of any particular group of voters cannot be known in advance, the need to appeal to the electors may at times take on the semblance of a guessing game. This level of uncertainty was very much in evidence when, in 1918, a large new element had been added to the electorate, one whose party preferences were almost entirely unknown. Moreover at this time the emergence of a women's party was something that was taken quite seriously (Pugh, 1992). For a number of years after 1918 therefore the major parties formulated their policies in an attempt to check any move towards such a party, and tried to present themselves as having a special appeal to women.

This sensitivity to women's issues was apparent in the election manifestos issued before the election of 1918. The coalition between the Conservatives and the Liberals, for example, announced their intention to remove all existing inequalities in the law as between men and women. The Labour Party went even further, referring to its record on women's suffrage before the war and declaring emphatically 'the Labour Party is the Women's Party'. It also promised women complete adult suffrage and equal pay. The result of the election, however, showed no evidence that the new women voters were impressed by these claims and the coalition achieved a major victory, winning 473 seats against the 57 won by the Labour Party (Craig, 1970).

During the next few years a number of measures were passed by the House of Commons which suggested that MPs and, to a lesser extent, the government remained conscious of the change in the gender of the electorate. Almost immediately a bill to allow women to sit in the House of Commons was passed with a large majority, a concession to women's rights which was important in principle although it was to be many years before more than a handful of women were able to take advantage of it. The next move came, not from the government, but from the Labour Party. In April 1919 it introduced a radical women's emancipation bill which, apart from removing all disqualifications against women holding civil and judicial appointments, would have given them equal suffrage rights and allowed them to sit and vote in the House of Lords. Although there was government opposition, the House of Commons itself was clearly in support and the bill passed its second reading without a vote (Hansard, 4 April 1919). At the third reading the government announced its intention of bringing in its own bill, but in spite of this Labour's bill was passed by the House of Commons, only to be defeated in the Lords (Hansard, 4 July 1919).

The government bill, introduced later in the year from the Lords, carefully avoided the more controversial elements in the original bill (Hansard, 27 October 1919). Not only was the equal suffrage clause omitted but also the clause admitting peeresses to the House of Lords. Their admission was vigorously opposed by the Lords themselves and their opposition continued until after the second world war. Even more limiting was a new clause which exempted women in the civil service from its ruling, bringing them instead under special orders of Council. During the debate a Conservative Member, Major Hills, moved an amendment to add discrimination on the ground of marriage to the terms of the bill. His objective, he told the House, was to remove the marriage bar from the civil service. Although his amendment was accepted by the House, the Solicitor General made it clear that in his view the marriage bar in the civil service must remain. The main criticism of the new bill related to the exemption of the civil service from the clauses of the bill but the government was determined not to give way on this issue, no doubt responding to pressure from the Treasury and from the civil service itself which was strongly opposed to any equality of treatment between men and women in its ranks (Zimmeck, 1984; Martindale, 1938).

In reviewing the debates on the Sex Discrimination (Removal) bill it is clear that at this time the House of Commons was more favourably disposed towards anti-discrimination legislation than was the government, which in spite of its election promises did very little, while in office, to redeem its pledge to remove existing legal inequalities between men and women. Nevertheless, it was prepared to yield to some extent to pressures from within the House of Commons and the Sex Discrimination (Removal) Act was the result. Although severely limited in its terms, especially by the exclusion of the civil service, it did allow women with certain exceptions to serve on juries, and to become magistrates, and it opened the legal profession to women. Nevertheless, as we have seen in previous chapters, Major Hills's amendment on marriage, although accepted by the House of Commons, in practice remained a dead letter, in spite of efforts to make use of it to end the marriage bar in the teaching profession.

In the House itself the issue of women in the civil service continued to occupy the attention of Members from both sides of the House (Hansard, 19 May 1920; 5 August 1921). The Orders in Council, when they were issued, discriminated against women severely, since they were not only selected in a different way from men but were placed in a different establishment. At the same time certain posts were retained for men alone. In spite of its critics the government would not give way, although it was forced to promise to review the situation at a later date, and subsequently some changes were made, so that by 1925 the position of women had to some extent improved (Martindale, 1938). Nevertheless it was not until after the second world war that such issues as equal pay, the end of the marriage bar, and the right of women to employment in all branches of the civil service were finally resolved.

Although the Labour Party must be given credit for its original anti-discrimination in 1919, its reputation as the Women's Party was severely tarnished by its support for the government's Restoration of Pre-war Practices Bill in the same year. The aim of the Act was simply to restore the prewar practices which had been held in abeyance during the war to allow women to work on machines previously the sole province of men, and was to redeem a promise made to the trade union movement during the war. Although a government bill, it had strong support from the Labour Party Members. The bill had strong support from the House, but there were some critics, the most notable being a Captain Loseby, a Conservative who claimed to be speaking for what he described as one of the largest women's organizations. He compared the refusal of the trade unions to allow women into certain jobs with the refusal of lawyers to admit women into the legal profession (Hansard, 2 June 1919).

If the Restoration of Pre-war Practices Act was passed against the wishes of the feminist organizations, other legislation passed during the life of the coalition government was more sympathetic to their aims. These included the Infanticide Act which removed the charge of murder for a woman guilty of killing her child where it was shown that she was suffering from the effects of her confinement, a Law of Property Act which placed mothers on an equal footing with fathers as to the inheritance of property from intestate children, as well as legislation to improve the position of women receiving maintenance from their husband. Perhaps the most important, because it was the subject of large-scale feminist campaigning, was the 1922 Criminal Law (Amendment) Act which not only raised the age of consent from 13 to 16 but, in certain circumstances, abolished the defence that a man had reasonable cause to believe that a girl was over the age of 16. Although concerned with the protection of young girls rather than with equal rights, it had been for many years an issue of great concern to women's organizations (Jeffreys, 1985).

In 1922 the postwar coalition came to an end and the government resigned. In the election manifestos of that year the Conservatives, perhaps confident that they already had the women's vote, made no mention of women, although the Labour and the Liberal Parties emphasized their concern for equal rights. In the event the Conservatives won handsomely. Their government, however, did not appear to be favourably disposed to women's rights and those MPs, both men and women, who put such issues forward were unsuccessful. Perhaps the greatest pressure at this time, both inside and outside Parliament, was for an extension of the suffrage which would give women equal rights with men. Attempts to introduce a private member's bill by Lord Robert Cecil, a Conservative and, later, by a Liberal, Isaac Foot, were received unsympathetically by the government (Hansard, 8 March 1922; 25 April 1923). Efforts to change the law with respect to women's rights as guardians of their children were also unsuccessful. The feminists did however achieve one notable success in 1923, with the passage of the Matrimonial Causes Act which allowed a wife equal grounds for divorce. This was a measure which the women's movement had sought for a very long time and the eventual success of the campaign owed a great deal to NUSEC and especially to Eva Hubback.

By 1923 the two women MPs, Nancy Astor and Margaret Wintringham, were beginning to take a major part in the discussion of women's issues, but with so very few women in the House men still played a leading part. Although, for example, Margaret Wintringham was prominent in the campaign for equal guardianship rights, she acted in partnership with both Colonel Greig, a Liberal, and Lieutenant Chilcott, a Conservative. In the campaign, waged in 1922 on behalf of women police by Nancy Astor and Margaret Wintringham, they were joined by Sir Arthur Steel Maitland, a Conservative. Men also figured largely in the pressure for equal suffrage.

More surprising is the extent of Conservative involvement in the pressure for women's rights and the low level of involvement on the part of Labour MPs, in spite of the emphasis on women's rights in Labour's election campaign. Moreover it is important to recognize that during these years Conservative MPs who pressed for women's rights, were pressuring their own government. While it is not possible to evaluate the motivation of these Conservative feminists, it strengthens the conclusion drawn in the previous chapters that gender was not a party issue.

At the end of 1923 there was another election, one which resulted in a Labour/Liberal coalition, although the Conservatives were still the largest party. Once again the Conservative manifesto made no mention of women, although both the Labour Party and the Liberals promised equal guardianship rights, and the Labour Party promised equal pay (Craig, 1970). Although only a minority government, Labour raised feminist hopes, especially in NUSEC (Alberti, 1989). However, for a number of reasons the feminists were destined to be disappointed. The coalition lasted for only nine months, giving the Labour Party little time to complete its plans; indeed several pieces of legislation were interrupted by the fall of the government in 1924. This was the case, for example, of a Summary Jurisdiction (Separation and Maintenance) Bill, designed to improve the position of separated wives, which was passed by the House of Commons and accepted by the House of Lords. Similarly, a bill to extend the franchise to all women was interrupted during its passage through the House of Commons. Again, although the government introduced a guardianship of infants bill in fulfilment of its election promise, this too was interrupted by the dissolution of Parliament. This bill, however, as we have seen in earlier chapters, was essentially a compromise bill which stopped well short of the equality demanded by the feminists and offered by the election manifestos of both the Labour and the Liberal Parties.

It has been suggested that the Labour government was half-hearted about the extension of the franchise (Alberti, 1989). Ramsay MacDonald did not include it in the King's speech and the bill to grant it was introduced, not by the government but by a Labour MP William Adamson. By the time the government was willing to take responsibility for it, it was too late. In the case of equal guardianship rights there was a clear lack of commitment displayed, not only in the timing of its introduction but, even more significantly, in the terms of the bill itself.

An even greater cause for dissatisfaction with Labour's period of office was the attitude shown by the government and the Party leadership to the demand on the part of Labour women for birth control information to be made available at local authority welfare centres. Their campaign was sparked off in 1922 by the dismissal of Nurse Daniels in Edmonton for providing this information, an action on the part of a local authority which led to a surge of protests on her behalf. An approach to the Ministry of Health merely confirmed Edmonton's action and it was ruled that women needing such assistance should obtain it privately. The issue was raised in the House of Commons by the Labour MP for Edmonton, F.A. Broad, but to no effect. The advent of a Labour government in 1924 raised hopes of a change of policy but they were dashed when in June a Ministry circular confirmed the prohibition. The issue was again raised in the House of Commons in July by two Labour MPs, Ernest Thurtle and Dorothy Jewson. The Labour Minister of Health, a Catholic, claimed in reply that the subject was too controversial (Hansard, 30 July 1924).

The end of 1924 saw a further election and this time it was the Conservative Party which made an appeal for the women's votes. Its manifesto listed a number of issues, including equal rights in guardianship, an amendment to the law relating to separation and maintenance orders, and an increase in the number of women police. In the election that followed the Conservatives were victorious and went on to hold the balance of power for the next four years. The Labour Party secured almost as many seats as in the previous election but the number of seats held by the Liberals declined dramatically, falling from 158 in 1923 to 40 in 1924.

The new government was responsible for several measures designed to appeal to women. The first of these was a guardianship of infants bill, which received its second reading on 4 March 1925 and its third on 8 April of that same year. This was not a new bill, since the Conservatives merely took over the bill introduced by the Labour government a year previously; it was essentially an attempt at a compromise between the feminist position and that of their opponents. It granted equal guardianship rights to women only when a married couple separated. While they were living together the husband was still the legal guardian and, in practical terms, the head of the household. Although the feminists were disappointed, many of them accepted the bill as a step forward, and Ellen Wilkinson, now in the House of Commons, welcomed it on those terms.

A second Act in 1925, the Summary Jurisdiction (Separation and Maintenance) Act, was another piece of legislation which had been interrupted by the dissolution. This extended the grounds on which either partner in a marriage could obtain a separation order and, of particular importance to women, abolished the requirement that a wife must leave her husband before applying for a separation order. That same year also saw the passage of the Widows, Orphans and Old Age Contributory Pensions Act, a piece of legislation which provided pensions for widows of insured men. Widows' pensions had been part of Labour Party policy for some years, and a long campaign had been conducted by the trade union movement. They were also included in the objectives of a very large variety of women's organizations, including equal rights groups as well as women in the labour movement. The legislation might therefore be counted as a victory for the women's cause.

Susan Pedersen has however recently cast doubts on such a supposition. She claims that widows' pensions were seen as an alternative to family endowment, a scheme which aroused much hostility within the labour and trade union movement because it appeared to threaten male wages. Moreover, family endowment was conceived as a payment to mothers, by virtue of their motherhood, whereas widows' pensions were seen by the labour movement as the right of a man to support for his wife and children when he could no longer support them himself. Widows' pensions posed no threat to the concept of the male breadwinner. Pedersen also points out that widows' pensions in themselves did nothing for women specifically as mothers. Not only were childless widows included in the scheme but many mothers were excluded because widows of uninsured men, deserted and separated wives, and unmarried mothers did not benefit (Pedersen, 1989).

The short-lived Labour government of 1924 failed to introduce any legislation on pensions and it was left to the Conservative government who, recognizing that some scheme was inevitable, tried to minimize its cost by making it a contributory scheme, based on insured male contributions. Indeed Labour was critical of the bill, objecting both to its contributory nature and to the low rates of pension. By making a limited concession to the demand for a pension scheme, the Conservative Party was able to take credit for the reform as well as ward off demands for non-contributory pensions and family allowances, both of which were judged as too expensive.

The Conservatives were also able to claim credit for granting an equal franchise to women, although this particular measure was delayed until almost the end of their period in office. The Prime Minister, Baldwin, did however disarm criticism in 1925 by promising a bill 'during the life-time of the present Parliament' and this promise was eventually fulfilled (Hansard, 29 March 1928). This particular government does therefore stand out for the extent of its concessions to the claims of the women's movement. At the same time it was quite prepared to reject other pressures, both from the women's movement itself and from within Parliament. In 1925 for example an attempt was made by two Conservative MPs, Major Halsey and Nancy Astor, to allow women, like men, to retain their British nationality on marriage but their claim was rejected by the government on the ground that they could do nothing without the consent of the self-governing Dominions. In spite of this argument the motion was carried by the House of Commons but no further action was taken at this time (Hansard, 18 February 1925).

In 1927 an attempt was made to introduce a Married Women's Employment Bill. Sponsored by NUSEC, it was aimed primarily at the marriage bar, and like the bill on nationality it was moved by a Conservative, Sir Robert Newman, although seconded by a Labour MP, Frederick Pethick-Lawrence, a former suffrage supporter. Other supporters from the Labour side included Ernest Thurtle and Sir H. Slesser who pointed to the limitations of the 1919 Sex Disqualification (Removal) Act as a reason for the proposal. In opposition to the bill a government spokesman pointed out that the bill might actually discourage the employment of women as well as act as an encouragement to women to neglect their home duties. Unlike the nationality bill, support from the House was not forthcoming and the issue was not raised again until during the war (Hansard, 29 April 1927).

The other feminist issue raised in the House during the lifetime of this government was birth control. By 1924 this had become a central issue amongst Labour women in spite of considerable opposition from the leadership of the Party, and the women's campaign enjoyed support from individual feminists and some feminist groups. In 1926 a Labour MP, Ernest Thurtle, tried to introduce a bill into the House to authorize local authorities to incur expenditure to convey birth control information when it was desired. He was strongly opposed by another Labour MP, a Mr Ball, who claimed that it was not Labour Party policy. In the voting that followed the bill was lost by 167 votes to 81, although a similar debate in the House of Lords shortly afterwards produced a victory, if a narrow one, for the birth control cause. The debate in the House of Commons revealed a Labour Party divided since no less than three men of cabinet rank, Snowden, Trevelyan and Lansbury, supported Thurtle. On the other hand only 27 Labour MPs voted in support, as compared with 54 Conservatives (Hansard, 9 February 1926; Douse and Peel, 1965). Nor, as we have seen, was it an issue which at this time commanded the support of women MPs in the House.

In attempts to understand the attitude of the Labour Party to birth control the opposition of the Catholic Church is crucial, since in some areas the Catholic vote was central to Labour's success in elections. The Party leadership may also have thought it divisive in other ways and this argument was used by Marion Phillips and later by Ramsay MacDonald. In 1928 Arthur Henderson managed to persuade the women's conference to reverse its previous position on birth control by appeals to party priorities in the light of the coming election. Clearly, therefore, the party stand was taken largely in the light of its perception of the electorate's hostility to birth control. On the other hand, there was also an ideological element. In the House of Commons, for example, Ball, in opposing Thurtle, argued that the solution to the problems faced by mothers with large families lay in the proper use of resources and not the limitation of births. Marion Phillips also made the same point when she argued that the task of the Labour Party was to redistribute wealth in such a way as to eliminate problems of over-population. There was no understanding here of the feminist arguments in favour of birth control.

In 1929 election manifestos still continued to pay attention to women. The Conservative emphasis however had moved away from equal rights and it focused mainly on health and welfare as they affected women and children. The Labour Party, on the other hand, still paid some attention to equal rights and argued that anomalies and injustice still remained and that the fight for women's emancipation was not yet finished. In the election that followed Labour for the first time was the party with the majority of seats in the House, although the now very small Liberal Party held the balance. Yet, in the admittedly short period in which Labour was in office, little was done for women. Indeed an attempt to change the law on the nationality of British women, supported by both Labour and Conservative MPs, was rejected on precisely the same grounds on which the Conservative government had rejected the same proposal in 1925 (Hansard, 28 November 1930).

It was, however, in connection with unemployment insurance that the Labour government came into most conflict with feminists both inside and outside the House. The source of the controversy was an attempt to reduce claims for unemployment benefit by married women claimants, whose numbers had increased markedly between 1927 and 1930. In order to claim, married women were required to prove that they were genuinely available for employment by the provision that they must have a record of work after their marriage (Hansard, 8 July 1931). Margaret Bondfield, the minister responsible for the legislation, defended her proposal on the ground that it was designed only to prevent women claiming unemployment benefit who had no intention of seeking work, but a number of women MPs were clearly unhappy with her argument and Eleanor Rathbone's unsuccessful attempt to amend the bill was supported by some women MPs in the Labour Party.

While in office however the Labour government relaxed its total opposition to the campaign to provide birth control information in local authority clinics. In 1930, with some local authorities threatening to defy the Ministry, the Minister of Health issued a circular which tried to contain the revolt by restricting birth control information to those women who needed it on medical grounds (Soloway, 1982). Clearly, therefore, the second Labour government, although it lasted longer in office, could only have been a disappointment to those feminists who still hoped that the Labour Party was serious in its election promises.

On the whole feminists looked back to the 1920s with satisfaction. Although by no means all their hopes were realized some of the long-standing aims of the women's movement relating to the suffrage, to divorce, and in a limited way equal guardianship, had been realized and there is no doubt that many individual feminists saw the decade of the 1920s as one of considerable success for their movement (Strachey, 1936). Moreover, as we have seen, the political parties had all taken notice of the women's vote in their election manifestos and, as Pugh has shown, the percentage of candidates who mentioned women in their own election manifestos remained high throughout the decade, in spite of variations between elections. The 1930s however were to be very different. Already in 1931 mention of women in candidates' election manifestos had dropped dramatically to a record low of 16 per cent (Pugh, 1992, p. 120). Indeed, Pugh himself argues that women's issues were 'pushed off the agenda' in 1931 (Pugh, 1992, p. 122). Clearly, therefore, if politicians had been apprehensive about the effect of the new women voters in 1918, they were no longer apprehensive by 1931.

The 1931 election produced a so-called national government with a total of 521 seats compared with only 52 seats for the Labour Party. Every woman Labour MP was defeated and there were ten new Conservative women, some of whom were later to emerge as feminists. The election itself had been dominated by the economic crisis and none of the party election manifestos made any mention of women. This lack of interest was manifest in the actions of the government itself so that, although women's issues did surface in the new Parliament, this was largely due to the efforts of a small group of women led by the Independent, Eleanor Rathbone. In 1932, for example, a decision to reduce women's sickness benefits was criticized by both Eleanor Rathbone and Nancy Astor, although Rathbone's attempt to defeat it was unsuccessful (Hansard, 14 June 1932). A week later an amendment which would have deprived a woman of benefit on marriage, leaving her to reinstate herself, was attacked by a group of Conservative women MPs, led by Nancy Astor and supported by the Labour Party. In the event, the government itself refused to support the amendment and it was lost (Gilbert, 1970).

The only action on women's issues taken by the government itself was a bill introduced in 1933 which made provision for those British women rendered stateless by marriage to retain their British nationality. This followed a League of Nations conference in The Hague in

1930 which recommended this change. Although recognizing that a large number of women's organizations wanted this right for all British women, the government took the view, as the Labour government had in 1930, that this could not be done without full Commonwealth agreement. Nancy Astor's protests were joined to those not only of Captain Cazalet, a Conservative, but also those of Clement Attlee in a stand which entirely reversed the view taken by Labour in 1930. The bill, however, received general support because it was recognized that it would give relief to those women who most needed it (Hansard, 9 November 1933).

In 1935 another election followed and another national government was elected, although with a smaller majority. Once more women's issues found little expression in any of the election manifestos and this was reflected in the actions of the government once in office. The only legislation aimed at reducing inequality between men and women was the Inheritance (Family Provision) Bill in 1938. Originally proposed by Rathbone, it sought to prevent a man leaving his inheritance away from his wife and family (Hansard, 29 April 1933).

Within the House of Commons the government was challenged on several occasions when it proposed legislation which was seen as discriminating. There was some, though unsuccessful, protest when the Contributory Pensions (Voluntary Contributions) Bill differentiated between men and women in terms of the income limit, which was much higher for men than for women (Hansard, 8 April 1937). It was the issue of equal pay in the civil service, however, which was most revealing of the lack of sympathy with which the leaders of the government treated women's claims. The question was raised in 1935 by Major Hills, a Conservative, whose support for equal pay in the civil service went back to 1919. Duff Cooper, Financial Secretary to the Treasury, replied by asserting that the civil service did not get the same value from women's work, citing their poorer health, their retirement on marriage and their lack of physical endurance (Hansard, 7 June 1935).

A year later Ellen Wilkinson, now back in the House, moved a resolution on equal pay in the civil service, which was seconded by Mr Jagger, a Labour MP from NUDAW. The Financial Secretary to the Treasury, in opposing the motion, gave a lengthy list of reasons against equal pay, ranging from the greater burden on men of marriage to the lack of discontent of women with their pay and the comparability of women's pay in the civil service with their pay outside. In spite of this opposition, the motion was carried, imposing a humiliating defeat on the government which was taken up vigorously by the opposition (Hansard, 1 April 1936). The Prime Minister, Baldwin, chose to make the issue one of confidence and in the ensuing division the motion was heavily defeated, since even those Members who strongly supported equal pay were not prepared to bring their own government down.

The 1930s were therefore unsuccessful for the women's movement, especially in comparison with the 1920s. This seems to have been in part at least a recognition by the parties that women would not unite on gender issues and could indeed be appealed to on the lines of orthodox party policies. It is also clear that in neither main party was there any serious commitment to a feminist ideology. Although prepared to approve a limited programme of equal rights, there was a consistent refusal to accept any feminist claim which appeared to threaten the traditional separation between men and women in both the home and the workplace.

As Pugh has pointed out, both parties shared a common belief in the traditional family and, in so far as they were interested in women's issues at all, looked with favour only on those which strengthened women's position as housewives and mothers (Pugh, 1992).

The 1930s also saw changes within the women's movement itself as the 'new' feminism challenged equal rights feminism for supremacy. The consequence was a switch of emphasis towards the needs of motherhood and the welfare of mothers and children, rather than the rights of women to justice. The decline of NUSEC too was a serious blow to the feminist movement since much of the 1920s legislation owed its success to NUSEC pressure and NUSEC lobbying. With NUSEC in decline, there was no one organization able to take its place (Doughan, 1980). This meant that just at the time that politicians were losing their fear of women voters, there was less pressure on them from the organized women's movement. When we add the crisis situation within the economy itself, which certainly distracted politicians in 1931, and the growing fears of an international crisis and the move towards war, it is not perhaps surprising that issues concerning women moved off the agenda.

The outbreak of war in 1939 prevented a further election, although in 1940 the national government was replaced by a coalition for the duration of the war. Labour now played an important role in government since several key figures, including Ernest Bevin at the Ministry of Labour, were drawn from the Labour Party. The war years also witnessed a resurgence of the feminist movement, especially on the issue of equal pay (Smith, 1981), and Harrison has argued that periods of coalition are on the whole favourable for the development of political feminism (Harrison, 1986). Yet, during the war there was little evidence of any real response on the part of either side in the coalition to demands from women inside or outside Parliament, and Smith has argued that the government made determined efforts to maintain pre-war practices of sexual differentiation (Smith, 1986).

The need for women's labour during the war did indeed secure some advantages for women. These included the temporary withdrawal of the marriage bar and, for those women replacing men in engineering, equal pay. However it appears that in practice employers frequently evaded paying such women equal wages, often by slight alterations to the work process so that it was no longer identical with that performed by men. Male workers at shop-floor level were also opposed to equal pay, giving rise to fears of industrial unrest if equal pay agreements were applied widely (Smith, 1981). There was also some provision of day nurseries but they were insufficient to meet women's needs. The Ministry of Health preferred 'minders' in spite of evidence that women's organizations, like the Women's Co-operative Guild and Labour women's sections, wanted nurseries. There was a reluctance to make changes in customary practices in such areas as shopping. Efforts to reduce the hours of work to make it easier for women to work were also resisted. Indeed there was a development of shift work and later part-time work (Summerfield, 1984). Although this met the needs of many women it also, as we have seen in previous chapters, had the effect of reinforcing the ideology of the centrality for women of work in the home.

In spite of certain wartime concessions in engineering the government policy on pay did a great deal actually to strengthen sex differentiation. Differences in pay between men and women were proposed in the armed forces, in civil defence and, as we have seen in an earlier chapter, in compensation for war injuries. There was also a system of unequal war bonuses in the civil service. Moreover, determined efforts were made by members of the government and especially by the Minister of Labour, Bevin, to prevent equal pay from ever becoming a political issue (Smith, 1981). The government was however helpless to prevent equal compensation becoming the subject of a large-scale campaign both inside and outside the House of Commons, a campaign which was ultimately so successful that it forced the government to give way.

Inside the House the campaign, which was fought mainly by women, emerged as early as 1939, and was remarkable for the degree of co-operation between women from both the main parties. At first, efforts to change the system of payment were unsuccessful, the government defending the scheme on the ground that it was based on average earnings which were lower for women (Hansard, 20 March 1941). Pressure continued however and finally in 1942 the government offered a select committee, although its terms of reference were deliberately framed to avoid all mention of equal pay (Smith, 1981). Finally, in 1943, it was announced that because the compensation referred only to injuries associated with war, there was no need for it to be related to earnings.

Undoubtedly, the pressure placed on the government was a significant factor in explaining its willingness to give way, especially since, by 1942, voting in the House of Commons had turned against the government on the issue (Hansard, 25 November 1942). Nevertheless, a vote against the government was not necessarily sufficient to force it to yield, and the fact that the issue of compensation could be contained within the limitation of a temporary war measure was probably of much more importance. Although this was certainly the greatest feminist victory of the war years, its significance should not be over-emphasized.

The campaign for equal pay did not arouse nearly as much feeling as did the campaign for equal compensation, perhaps because the inequalities in compensation were presented in a rather blatant form, with single men receiving much more than single women, and married men in addition qualifying for grants for dependent children, thus making irrelevant one of the arguments in favour of unequal pay. Nevertheless there was pressure for equal pay both inside and outside Parliament and Edith Summerskill even went so far as to oppose conscription of women if equal pay was not provided (Smith, 1986). Moreover, like equal compensation, the struggle was not confined to any one party. In 1944 when the Conservative feminist, Thelma Cazalet-Keir, moved an amendment to the education bill which would have given equal pay to teachers, she was seconded by another Conservative, Major Thorneycroft (Hansard, 28 March 1944). The amendment was accepted by the House but rejected by the government who, determined not to give way, used the same device that had been used in

1936, with similar success. Even Thelma Cazalet-Keir felt it necessary to vote against her own amendment rather than face the resignation of Churchill, whom she much admired, and the wartime government (Hansard, 29 March 1944). The next step in the government's determined opposition was the delaying tactic of a Royal Commission, and this had the desired effect, postponing further discussion on equal pay until the war was over (Smith, 1981).

Another issue which found the coalition government facing a revolt by women MPs of both parties was the payment of family allowances. It was clear that the government, influenced by the Treasury, wanted them paid to the father. It was suggested by Butler, for example, that since the father was the breadwinner he, and not the mother, was entitled to claim the allowance (Hansard, 3 November 1944). The bill itself was a compromise, suggesting that the allowance could be cashed by either parent, but this solution aroused so much anger from women's organizations, as well as from women in the House including Eleanor Rathbone, that it was finally agreed that the money should go to the mother (Land, 1975; Macnicol, 1980). It was clear from the debate however that the government had no sympathy for the feminist arguments involved.

The need for women's labour during the war had brought an end to the marriage bar in both teaching and the civil service, but it was made clear that this was a temporary concession only. During the debate on the Education Bill in 1944 a proposal to end the marriage bar in teaching was made by a Conservative, Hamilton Kerr. The Board of Education wanted it to stay but Chuter Ede, a Labour MP and at that time Parliamentary Secretary to the Board, argued that it should go not, as he carefully pointed out, on 'negative' feminist grounds, but because of his dislike of what he called 'sex starved spinsters' as teachers. There was also anxiety on the part of the government about a future teacher shortage and the amendment, abolishing the marriage bar, was accepted and became part of the Education Act. The shortage of women clerks also led to the lifting of the marriage bar in the civil service a few years later (Smith, 1984a). This was an important victory for the women's movement which had long opposed the imposition of the bar as an infringement of a married woman's right to work, but its final abolition had little to do with feminist arguments or even with feminist pressure.

On the whole therefore the wartime coalition did not provide a favourable setting for the success of feminist goals. Such concessions as were made were largely of a limited nature and designed quite deliberately to last only for the duration of the war. Even the lifting of the marriage bar was intended to be temporary and the fact that it was not reimposed was mainly a consequence of the economic boom which came at the end of the war. The successful campaign to achieve equal compensation for wartime injuries led, as the government well realized, to only a temporary concession which had no effect on the long-term goal of equal pay. In spite of the resurgence of feminist activity both inside and outside Parliament, it was unable to make much headway against the determination of the government to maintain prewar sex differentiation.

The wartime coalition came to an end in 1945, and in the election that followed a Labour landslide brought the Labour Party into power with a large majority. There was now an opportunity for Labour to show itself as the Women's Party, as it had previously claimed and as some of its supporters still believed it to be. However, the Labour Party no longer seemed to want to make such a claim. Indeed, on women's issues the Conservative and Labour manifestos bear a striking resemblance (Craig, 1970). The Conservative manifesto, for example, argued that 'motherhood must be our special care'. Mention was made of an increase in maternity beds and of encouragement of nursery schools and nurseries. Family life, it was argued, was a precious asset to be defended at all costs. Labour, too, in its manifesto emphasized the family, arguing that parenthood must not be penalized if the population of Britain was to be prevented from dwindling. There was special mention of school medical and feeding services and better provision for maternity and child welfare. There was no reference to the fight for women's emancipation, as there had been for example in 1929, nor, as there had been then, any promise of equal treatment for men and women. Most significant of all there was no mention of equal pay.

In 1946 the Royal Commission on Equal Pay issued its report which was on the whole equivocal. While accepting the claims of women in the professions, in the civil service and in teaching, it argued that women in manual employment did not make an equal contribution, citing such failings as lesser strength, greater absenteeism, and lack of flexibility. Only three commissioners, all women, disagreed with this assessment of women's work. On women in the civil service and in teaching, however, the message was clear and when the government made no move to implement this part of the report, there was considerable disappointment in the labour movement and this manifested itself at the annual conference of the Labour Party in 1947. Eirene White, later to become a prominent feminist MP, moved a motion calling for the immediate implementation of equal pay which, although opposed by the national executive, was carried by an overwhelming majority (Meehan, 1990). Even faced with this kind of pressure from its own party, the government refused to give way and the implementation of equal pay was rejected out of hand during the whole of the government's period of office.

The Labour government was equally unmoved by pressure from its own party within the House of Commons, which surfaced from time to time in spite of pressure from the leadership to stifle criticism from its ranks (Pugh, 1992). At the same time the trade union movement was persuaded to back-pedal its own demands for equal pay (Lewenhak, 1977). The government used the state of the economy and particularly the danger of inflation to explain its refusal even to discuss the implementation of equal pay, but there were clear signs that this preoccupation with the economy was not the only reason for its attitude. There was a lack of sympathy with the concept of equal rights in general and this was made very clear in the 1945 manifesto with its emphasis on mothers and motherhood. Indeed it is likely that for the Labour leadership at this time its concept of itself as a women's party was based on the general provisions of the welfare state. In 1950 for example equal pay was linked specifically to the development of the social services and women were warned that, because of the benefits available to women under the welfare state, they would be unwise to press for equal pay, in case these benefits were to be placed in jeopardy (Hansard, 2 November 1950).

The attitude to equal pay, therefore, depended fundamentally on the concept of the husband as breadwinner and his wife as his dependent, a concept which gave very little attention to the woman in employment, whether she was married or single. The argument for equal pay, and indeed equal rights generally, cut right across this particular ideology because it emphasized women not simply as wives and mothers but as independent persons. To the labour movement on the other hand and within the concept of the welfare state, especially as it was developed by Beveridge, women were not individuals in their own right but a part, and indeed a subordinate part, of a family system. In many ways the ideology of the welfare state was an economic version of the legal system which in the nineteenth century denied a married woman any legal rights at all.

On the whole, then, the Labour administration failed to introduce any legislation of significance to give women greater equality or greater independence. The benefits they achieved under the welfare state served rather to emphasize their dependence. Two measures must however, be singled out as exceptions. In 1948 a government bill made it possible at long last for women to retain their British citizenship on marriage (Hansard, 7 July 1948). In 1946, following a recommendation in the Gowers Report, it was announced that women were now to be allowed to enter the foreign service, although with a general marriage bar that could be waived in special circumstances (Hansard, 20 March 1946). On the other hand, a motion in 1949 to admit peeresses to the House of Lords was blocked by the Labour Party who objected to what they saw as a strengthening of the hereditary principle.

Another election in 1950 again returned Labour to power but with only a small majority. In their manifestos both parties made a promise of equal pay, in the case of Labour for women generally, in the case of the Conservatives only for women in the government services. However by offering 'an early date' the Conservatives stole a march on Labour who merely promised 'when the nation's circumstances allow it' (Craig, 1970). Nevertheless, during its brief spell in office the Labour government found itself under considerable pressure to implement some measure of equal pay without delay. In August 1951, for example, a Labour MP, Douglas Houghton, introduced a motion in his name which included the signatures of about 70 other Members of all parties. Speaking on behalf of the government, Douglas Jay rejected the motion (Hansard, 2 August 1951).

It is possible that, had they remained in office, the government might have responded to what was a great degree of pressure and made at least some concessions to the equal pay campaign within their own party and within the trade union movement. Instead, by the end of 1951 the Conservatives were again in power. This increased the pressure inside the House since Labour MPs, now in opposition, felt free to speak their minds. The arguments for equal pay did not however come only from Labour MPs and in 1954 Douglas Houghton introduced a bill which had the support of both sides of the House (Hansard, 9 March 1954). At first the government resisted the pressures but in April 1954 Butler announced that talks were in progress with the national staff side of the civil service (Hansard, 6 April 1954), and details of the final scheme were given to Parliament in January 1955 (Hansard, 27 January 1955). Later, teachers and other groups were added.

Undoubtedly, the reason for the decision to yield to the campaign for equal pay in the civil service was a political one. By yielding the government was able to claim credit for a measure which had traditionally been regarded as a substantive part of Labour Party policy, a tactic which they had of course used with success in the years before the second world war. Moreover, as Pugh points out, a key factor was the next election. They had won narrowly in 1951 and must have seen equal pay as a way to outflank the opposition in 1955 (Pugh, 1992).

It is less easy to understand how the Labour government allowed itself to be outflanked in this way. One possible explanation is that it was easier for ideological reasons for a Conservative government to limit equal pay to civil servants and teachers than for a Labour government to do so. By imposing such a limitation the Conservatives made it very much easier for themselves both financially and administratively but a Labour administration might have felt uneasy about the exclusion of the much larger number of women manual workers who would not benefit at all. Yet they were clearly unwilling to commit themselves to the much more difficult and indeed much more problematic measure which they eventually introduced in 1970.

Shortly after the announcement of the phased introduction of equal pay there was another election. In their manifestos neither the Labour Party nor the Conservative Party made any promises to women, although the Conservatives made a point of reminding the electors of their action on equal pay. Whether for this or for other reasons, they were returned with an even larger majority. This administration made male soliciting an offence, an important equal rights measure even if not directly applicable to women. It was also responsible for one important measure which had been a goal of the women's movement for many years. The bill, a maintenance order bill, improved the machinery for paying maintenance to divorced and separated wives, and was introduced because of the cost to the National Assistance Board of the growing number of divorces and separations. One particular innovation, which women had been asking for since the 1920s (Brophy, 1982), was the attachment of earnings for maintenance arrears, a measure which had always been opposed by the Labour Party in case it might lead to difficulties for a man in his employment. Indeed, the Labour Party seems to have had little sympathy for the attempts at this time to improve the financial position of deserted and separated wives, and although Edith Summerskill, a Labour MP, was a leading figure in this campaign, she does not seem to have been given much support within her own party. This may have been a consequence of the largely male orientation of the whole of the labour movement.

Another election, in 1959, again returned the Conservatives to power. The only mention of women in the parties' election manifestos was a promise by Labour to review widows' pensions. Nor was the administration itself concerned with women's issues. Indeed, the passage of the Street Offences Bill in 1959 continued the pattern of discrimination against prostitutes and even to some extent worsened their position. It was accepted by a large majority within the House of Commons, including women MPs, and, as a previous chapter showed, only a small group of mainly Labour women argued against it on the ground that it discriminated against women. The only success of this administration so far as women were concerned was the attempt led by Barbara Castle to abolish turnstiles in public lavatories. This attempt had the backing of a large number of women's organizations and much support in the House of Commons (Hansard, 19 July 1961). Within a very few months local authorities were asked to remove existing turnstiles as soon as possible.

The next election, in 1964, brought a Labour victory for the first time since 1950. With the exception of help for widows, mentioned by both parties, there was no special mention of women in the manifestos, and certainly no indication that the decade of the 1960s was to see an eventual transformation in the women's movement. The Labour administration which followed lasted only two years but another election, in 1966, secured a larger majority which kept Labour in power until 1970. These six years of a Labour government broke the pattern of indifference to women's issues on the part of the Labour Party and to some extent redeemed its reputation as the Women's Party.

Almost from the first, in 1964, the government was under pressure both inside and outside the House on the issue of abortion. A revitalized Abortion Law Reform Association was gaining increasing support, and in the House of Commons the issue was raised by Labour MPs Renee Short and William Hamilton. Although Alice Bacon, the Minister of State at the Home Office, could not promise government legislation, she did suggest it as a topic for a private member's bill to test the opinion of the House (Hansard, 8 July 1965). The following year the Medical Termination of Pregnancy Bill was successfully piloted through the House by the Liberal MP, David Steel. The government, proclaiming its attitude to be neutral, nevertheless helped the bill by allowing a free vote (Hansard, 22 July 1966). This was in sharp contrast to the first of such bills, introduced by a Labour MP, Joseph Reeves, in 1952, which was opposed by his own party (Hindell and Simms, 1971). Another related success was Edwin Brooks's bill to provide family planning as part of the national health service. Kenneth Robinson, Minister of Health from 1964 to 1968, was supportive, and fears of overpopulation, current at that time, may have secured a sympathetic House of Commons (Leathard, 1980).

There was also pressure from Joyce Butler, a Co-operative and Labour MP, for legislation on the right of a deserted wife to remain in the matrimonial home (Hansard, 2 June 1965), and from the Conservative feminist, Joan Vickers, on guardianship rights for a deserted wife (Hansard, 7 April 1965). Then in 1968 Joyce Butler made the first of several attempts by MPs of both parties to secure an anti-discrimination bill to protect women against discrimination (Hansard, 7 March 1968).

Meanwhile, the demand for some kind of legislation on equal pay was mounting. The government had pledged itself to equal pay but showed little inclination to press ahead in spite of an attempt in 1968 to bring an equal pay bill before the House of Commons. Even as late as 1970 there seems to have been hesitation within the cabinet, with Crossman opposed and Jenkins anxious about costs (Carter, 1988). The final introduction of a bill that year seems to have been in part the influence of Barbara Castle and in part the action of Frank Cousins, General Secretary of the Transport and General Workers' Union, who threatened the government with the possibility of a trade union revolt on the issue (Lewenhak, 1977). Harold Wilson, the Prime Minister, also seems to have backed Barbara Castle within the cabinet (Carter, 1988). The last important piece of legislation was the Matrimonial Proceedings and Property Bill. This was introduced as a result of the Divorce Reform Act and was intended to protect the first wife in the case of a man's divorce and remarriage.

In order to understand why this Labour government should have been willing to accept measures to which it had previously been so resistant it is necessary to take account of the pressures which had been building up throughout the 1960s. In the trade union movement between 1964 and 1970, for example, women accounted for 70 per cent of the increase in the membership of trade unions affiliated to the

TUC and during this period, too, the women's advisory committee began to reflect the growing importance of women workers. This new militant mood increased its strength from 1968 (Boston, 1980; Lewenhak, 1977). Moreover by the end of the 1960s the new women's movement was beginning to influence women in the trade union movement. Within the Labour Party there was a general rise in militancy amongst women members and by the end of the decade in particular this was having its effect on women in Parliament. By the 1960s indeed some Conservative women were beginning to change, although Campbell suggests that feminism did not have an impact until the 1980s (Campbell, 1987).

It seems, on the whole, that it was this pressure which influenced the Labour government rather than any radical change of heart amongst its leaders. Legislation was rarely at the government's own instigation and even though the equal pay bill was introduced by the government there was doubt, and even some opposition within the cabinet. Wilson seems to have been a supportive figure in general but his own account of his administration, although lengthy and detailed, pays little attention to women's issues (Wilson, 1974). Stetson has argued that Labour MPs themselves played a predominant role. They tended to be young, middle-class, well-educated and nineteen of them were women. These young men and women thought such issues as abortion, homosexuality and divorce as important as nationalization. There had also been a new attitude in the House of Lords as a result of the Life Peerages Act of 1958 (Stetson, 1982).

In 1970 there was another election and both parties showed themselves immediately responsive to the new mood amongst women. After an almost total neglect of women's rights issues since 1929 both election manifestos revealed a new enthusiasm for women's emancipation. The Conservative Party promised not only to change the tax system but to end the anomalies in family law, and to bring in anti-discrimination legislation. For its part Labour promised that women should have the same rewards and opportunities as men (Craig, 1975).

Once in office however the Conservatives, who won the election, were less enthusiastic. Joyce Butler's anti-discrimination bill, moved on this occasion by William Hamilton (Hansard, 28 January 1972), was talked out by a group of Tory MPs. In the House of Lords an identical bill, introduced by Baroness Seears, was given a second reading, despite opposition from the government, and passed to a select committee. When the bill was introduced into the House of

Commons, the Minister of State for the Home Office was now willing to give his support in principle but asked for a delay to wait for the select committee's report. In spite of his intervention the bill passed its second reading (Hansard, 14 February 1973), but made no further progress.

The government did however fulfil its election promise on women's guardianship rights. A bill was introduced into the House of Lords and subsequently into the House of Commons which, for the first time, gave men and women equal rights over their children. This ended a legislative battle which had begun in 1839 with Caroline Norton's campaign to give mothers greater rights over their children. The Conservative Party was therefore able to claim the credit, although Joan Vickers, herself a Conservative, pointed out that it had been Conservatives who had talked the bill out in 1965 (Hansard, 8 May 1973).

In 1974 there were two elections, one in February and one in October. With the new women's movement by then at its height women's rights had a major part to play in the manifestos of the two parties. Anti-discrimination legislation was promised by both of them but the Labour Party also emphasized equal opportunities in education, training and employment, as well as new measures in social security, national insurance and taxation. The October election ushered in the last Labour administration before the long Conservative reign which began in 1979. Its most important piece of legislation was the Sex Discrimination Act of 1975 which attempted to outlaw discrimination against women, especially in the field of employment. Also of significance for women's rights was the Social Security Act of 1974. Like the Equal Pay Act it was largely the responsibility of Barbara Castle and made a serious attempt to move away from the doctrine of 'dependency' which had dominated the social security system since Beveridge.

In looking at the record of the two main parties it is obvious that neither of them can claim to be a women's party, if by that is meant making any serious commitment to the issues raised by the women's movement. Although both parties can claim credit for legislation which met the demands of the movement, such legislation was on the whole yielded only grudgingly and as a result of long and arduous campaigns. Frequently indeed both parties appeared to be not simply indifferent to those issues raised by the women's movement, but actually hostile.

In some respects the Labour Party appears to have a greater claim to the title. Its own women's movement certainly showed a greater concern for feminist issues than Conservative women and the radical reformist ideology of the labour movement also gave credence to the belief, shared by many feminists, that they would have more sympathy with the desire to bring greater equality to the relationship between men and women just as they wished to bring it to men and women of different economic classes. As we have seen, however, Labour governments frequently had to share credit with Conservative administrations, which have shown themselves alert to the political advantage of responding to pressure for reform on a variety of issues, ranging from equal suffrage to equal pay. At the same time there were feminists in both parties, both male and female, and it would be hard to demonstrate that either party had a monopoly of them.

On the other hand, the Labour Party does seem to have offered more opportunities to women both to enter Parliament, and once in Parliament to hold office. In the 50 years between 1920 and 1970 47 of women MPs represented Labour, 31 the Conservatives, four the Liberals, and one was an Independent. The first woman minister was appointed by Labour in 1929 but the Conservatives did not appoint a woman minister until 1951. Harold Wilson, certainly the prime minister who did most for women, appointed two women to full government positions between 1974 and 1976, Barbara Castle and Shirley Williams. In this respect at least therefore Labour showed a commitment to equal rights not shared by the Conservative Party.

Nevertheless, the fact that there were more women representing the Labour Party in the House of Commons, while potentially of significance to the women's movement, depended on the extent to which they were prepared to commit themselves to issues of gender which cut across party lines and party loyalties. Although some Labour women in Parliament were active feminists, there were others who undoubtedly put party issues first. This led them to try not to rock the boat so far as their own party was concerned, and they remained loyal backbenchers, accepting the party line on gender as on all other issues.

There is evidence however that by the 1960s this had changed. Labour women in the House began to take an increasingly feminist line on gender issues and this reached a peak in the early 1970s under the influence of the new feminist movement. Interestingly this feminist consciousness seems to have crystallized most strongly, not around the anti-discrimination legislation, but around the attempt by James White to amend the original Abortion Act of 1967 to make abortions more difficult. All but two of the women in the House and all the women

Labour MPs supported the original Act, and the feeling that the limitations on the original Act were being imposed by men on women led to what Vallance has called an 'unprecedented unity' (Vallance, 1979).

The women's movement has therefore been a highly significant part of the political pressure on Parliament and particularly on governments in forcing concessions on issues of feminist concern. It is clear indeed, from the part played by such issues in party policy, that they were never genuine party issues and, for this reason, never played anything but a subsidiary role in the political process, which has depended upon the struggle between the two major parties. Instead both parties competed with each other to find favour with women voters and both parties, at different times, were able to claim credit for particular concessions, so that in this way party rivalry could sometimes work to the advantage of the women's movement.

Although, therefore, it can be argued that the political context was significant for both successes and failures of the women's movement during the period between 1920 and the early 1970s, it was perhaps less important than the economic context in explaining the attitude of successive governments to gender issues. To some extent this has been touched on in earlier chapters but it is the purpose of the following, and final substantive chapter, to look at the economic context in detail, and to examine its relationship both with politics and with ideology, as well as the ways in which it related back to the nature of feminism itself.

7.   The Economic Context

Among the various factors which influenced the reception of the proposals advocated by the women's movement, the state of the economy was of great importance. This did not apply in every case and sometimes, as for example the extension of the franchise, the political circumstances were much more significant. In certain other campaigns however the economic context played a key role. Moreover the most important aspect of the economy during the period of this study was the employment market, both in terms of the general level of unemployment for both men and women and more specifically in terms of the demand for women's labour. During the first world war women had been needed to replace men sometimes in jobs which had previously been entirely a male preserve, and women were drawn into the labour market in unprecedented numbers. Once the war was over however the needs of ex-servicemen were regarded as paramount and the end of the war saw the exodus of large numbers of women from the workforce. Moreover the early 1920s, marked as they were by a severe slump, witnessed the rise of the accusation that women were taking men's jobs. Nor was this accusation entirely without substance. Although the trade unions continued to control many skilled jobs through their hold over apprenticeship, new automated processes in industry outside such control were bringing in large numbers of women at lower rates of pay (Boston, 1980). In the white-collar sector, although professional women made few gains at this time (Adam, 1975), women clerks not only maintained the gains they had made during the war but continued to increase in numbers (Roberts, 1988). Like women in manual work however they worked for less pay than men.

On the other hand, this did not mean that women were untouched by the depression. The decline in the textile industry affected them very badly and many skilled women lost their jobs. Domestic service, in contrast, at that time the largest single area of women's work, did not suffer from unemployment at all and there was, instead, a constant and unfulfilled demand for domestic servants, both in private homes and in institutions. The existence of these vacancies led to numerous efforts to direct unemployed women, whatever their previous experience, into domestic work by withholding unemployment pay (Lewenhak, 1977; Roberts, 1988). Domestic workers themselves however were not insured against unemployment because it was not judged to be necessary. Although there were many protests at the way in which women, especially skilled workers, were being forced into domestic service it was accepted by the trade union and labour movement as necessary in the circumstances (Lewis, 1984; Boston, 1980). One consequence of this policy was that women's claims for unemployment benefit were much more likely to be disallowed than claims made by men. In the early 1920s for example 34 per cent of women's claims were disallowed, compared with only 13 per cent for men (Lewenhak, 1977). Women's sickness claims were also under attack, since it was alleged that they were too high. Under the Health Insurance and Contributory Pensions Act of 1932 benefits for both single and married women were reduced considerably (Gilbert, 1970).

It is against this background that we must understand the failure of feminist policies in the late 1920s and throughout the 1930s. Harrison, for example, argues that the depression helped to produce an anti-feminist reaction (Harrison, 1987), a point also made by Pugh (Pugh, 1990), who sees the decline in legislative progress for women after the early 1920s in these terms. Undoubtedly, whenever there was competition between men and women for jobs, the effect of male unemployment was to harden trade union attitudes to women workers, and it increased the likelihood that they would cling to traditional practices which excluded women. The use of women as cheap labour, which was widespread in both clerical work and in many new industrial processes, also increased trade union antagonism and may well help to explain the lack of enthusiasm within the labour movement for many feminist demands, in spite of its formal adherence to sex equality.

It was however the married women who suffered most from this hostility to working women, since it was recognized that single women had to support themselves. Married women were held to be the responsibility of their husbands, and the belief was widely held that it was wrong for two wages or salaries to go into one home. This belief was a factor in the imposition of marriage bars not only in the civil service and in teaching but in the textile industry where, in the 1930s, there was an attempt to replace married women with men. This caused a great deal of resentment among the women concerned and led unusually to a measure of cooperation between the textile women workers and the feminist Open Door Council and Six Point Group, who in 1933 spearheaded a campaign on the right of all married women to work (Liddington, 1984). The marriage bar in teaching was not imposed in the interests of men but was an attempt, mainly successful, to replace married women with recently trained young women teachers who were unable to find work, but it was still based on the same argument that married women did not have the same need to work. Indeed this point was raised as early as 1921 by the Chancellor of the Exchequer with respect to women in the civil service (Hansard, 5 August 1921). That this was very widely believed, even by some feminists, is confirmed by Edith Summerskill's confession in 1954 that she too had believed that at a time of high unemployment spinsters should have preference over married women because two wages should not go into one home (Hansard, 14 December 1954).

The marriage bar was also seen by employers as a useful way of maintaining a high level of staff mobility in jobs of a routine nature. By this device salaries were kept low and a supply of cheap labour was guaranteed. This was also behind the Treasury support for the marriage bar, and was part of their view of a civil service in which high-level posts were reserved for men, and women were confined to the lower levels in low-paid routine work (Zimmeck, 1984). Precisely the same conception can also be found in the Report of the Royal Commission on Equal Pay (Wilson, 1980).

It was the Anomalies Act of 1931 which demonstrated perhaps the most obvious example of discrimination against married women. The ostensible purpose of this Act was simply to eliminate fraud since it was claimed that married women who had no intention of returning to work were fraudulently claiming unemployment pay. Women were therefore excluded from benefit unless they had actually been at work since their marriage. This provision meant a great deal of hardship in areas like textiles where women had traditionally expected to work after marriage but where jobs were now not available because of the recession. It also appears to have been applied with exceptional severity and, although it was intended to deal with only a small number of cases of fraud, the number of women whose claims were disallowed was very high. In 1934, for example, Eleanor Rathbone pointed out that in the first fortnight after the Act was in force 74 000 women were struck off and in the first year 180 000 (Hansard, 24 April 1934). Clearly therefore the operation of the Act, like the marriage bar itself, was part of a belief that the support of a married woman was properly the responsibility of a husband and not the state.

The depression also had far-reaching effects on the campaign for equal pay. Although the arguments against equal pay were very varied, the claim that the country could not afford it was a very powerful one and could be used effectively even by those who claimed to approve of equal pay in principle. It was for example the reason given by Philip Snowden as Labour Chancellor in 1924, when he maintained that 'under existing conditions this very large expenditure cannot be faced' (Hansard, 6 August 1924). The opposition of the Treasury to equal pay in the civil service was also based on the state of the country's finances during the interwar depression years (Martindale, 1938). Apart from its initial cost, it was argued that it would lead to demands by men for more pay (Hansard, 1 April 1936). Indeed this fear that men would demand wage increases to restore their differential was to continue to be raised not only in the 1920s and 1930s but during and after the second world war. In consequence the demand for equal pay was seen not only as expensive in itself but as threatening the whole structure of earnings.

More serious even than the cost argument because it attacked the whole principle of equal pay was the claim, made frequently during this period, that women's lower pay was justified by their lower productivity: they were not performing equal work even in what appeared to be the same jobs. In justification of this claim it was argued, for example, that they had a higher sickness rate and less physical endurance, a critique of women's work which appeared not only from time to time in Hansard (Hansard, 7 June 1935, 3 August 1943), but in the Royal Commission on Equal Pay in 1946. Even Beatrice Webb in 1918 had assumed that women were inferior workers and also that for this reason equal pay would drive them out of their jobs (Lewis, 1984). This belief led to some ambivalence amongst women workers about the equal pay campaign (Lewenhak, 1977).

For the employers, of course, equal pay was a serious threat to their profitable use of women as cheap labour, and it is no surprise to find that they were the most consistent and determined of the opponents of any system of equal pay. It was for example the employers' side, both in the civil service and in teaching, which persisted in its opposition to equal pay even when the staff side was strongly in its favour (Partington, 1976). Similarly, employers' representatives, in their evidence to the Royal Commission on Equal Pay after the second world war, main-

tained their hostility, claiming not only that women were inferior workers but that equal pay would be economically ruinous. Their adherence
to the principle of low wages for women was however clearly to their
economic advantage and their persistent belief in the inferiority of
women's labour may well have been no more than special pleading.
Their evidence was nevertheless taken very seriously by the Commission and the final report to a considerable extent reflected their opinion
(Summerfield, 1984).

The desire of the employers to maintain women workers as a source
of cheap labour and their opposition to equal pay as a threat to this
policy were however a powerful incentive to trade unionists' support
of the equal pay campaign. As we have seen, although trade union
control over much traditional skilled work remained, there were important areas in both non-manual and manual employment where the
use of women as cheap labour was expanding. Increasingly, therefore,
equal pay began to seem an essential strategy to combat the threat of
cheap labour posed to men's wages and to men's jobs. This seems to
have occurred most strongly in clerical work and during the 1930s the
male leaders in white-collar unions moved towards equal pay as the
best solution to the increasing feminization of their work. The Union
of Post Office Workers, for example, were seriously alarmed by this
time at the way in which women were taking over men's jobs and,
although previously they had opposed equal pay in the belief that it
would interfere with the privileged position of the male worker, by the
mid-1930s equal pay began to be seen as a way of destroying the
management's incentive to employ women cheaply.

This change of attitude had nothing to do with feminism. Indeed, in
the interwar years the union endorsed the management policy of restrictions on the employment of both unmarried mothers and divorced
women (but not divorced men). The union was also fully behind the
marriage bar (Grint, 1988). The acceptance of the women's claim for
equal pay was based on the belief that it would lead to a loss of jobs
for women, who would be replaced by male workers, a loss justified
by their acceptance of an ideology that saw a woman's place as in the
home rather than at work.

The economic climate of the 1920s and 1930s also did a great deal
to consolidate and reinforce the traditional belief in the concept of the
family wage. This was not only of great importance as an aspect of
wage bargaining but was also very closely bound up with the construc-
tion of notions of masculine identity (Pedersen, 1989). The mass un-

employment of the period was a serious threat not only to the economic status of the male worker but to his position as breadwinner, and it is not surprising that there was trade union opposition to any feminist demand which seemed to place his role as head of the family in jeopardy.

In this context it becomes easier to understand the ambiguities in the trade union attitude to equal pay. Although it was welcomed as a way to discourage the use of women as cheap labour, it was also seen as a threat to the male worker's right to a higher wage because he was, at least potentially, a husband and father. Although, as we have seen, other arguments were used, a man's greater financial responsibilities were perhaps the most widely accepted. Indeed it was endorsed by many feminists, including Eleanor Rathbone, who believed that any provision for equal pay should be accompanied by a generous system of family allowances. At the same time the trade union belief in the concept of the family wage led them to oppose family allowances right through the 1920s and 1930s (Macnicol, 1980). It was believed within the labour and trade union movement that family allowances concealed an attack on wages and Ellen Wilkinson, for example, who had been one of the campaign's earliest supporters, later turned against it for precisely this reason. There was strong support from the women's sections as early as 1921 but, as with several other issues, the labour women were unable to persuade the movement as a whole. Pedersen has suggested that the women's views were diverted if not actually suppressed with the active assistance of Marion Phillips, then Chief Woman Officer of the Labour Party. Indeed, in this as in other cases women in the Party were caught between their loyalty to issues of gender and their loyalty to the movement.

On the whole, the preference within the Labour Party itself was for universal services rather than a cash allowance and it was argued that such allowances should only be given in the case of a father's failure to provide for his wife and children. In this way the right of the husband to seek a family wage was preserved. Pedersen suggests that the demand for family allowances was converted into a pressure for widows' pensions. In the process however the concept of pensions for mothers was swept away. Widows' pensions were not only paid to widows without children but many mothers were ineligible for a widows' pension, either because they were unmarried or because their husbands were not insured. Indeed it was made quite clear in the House of Commons that a widows' pension was a man's right, paid for by his contributions, and not a woman's right at all (Hansard, 30 June 1925). In this way the economic dependency of a wife on her husband was maintained both ideologically and in practice.

The failure of the women's movement during the late 1920s and the 1930s cannot, therefore, be entirely attributed to the weaknesses within the movement itself. These existed, it is true, but the campaigns of the period were fought in a hostile economic climate in which unemployment dominated the thoughts of government and opposition alike. Within this economic context women's claims were seen at best as trivial and unimportant, and at worst as actual threats to the country's economic well-being. This was particularly true of attempts by the feminists to improve women's opportunities at work, since the working woman was seen as a rival to the working man. Under these circumstances it is not surprising that neither in Parliament nor outside was it possible to build an alliance between feminism and the male-oriented labour and trade union movement in spite of considerable support for feminist goals from women's groups within the movement.

By 1940 the economic background had begun to change radically. Not only was unemployment ceasing to be a problem but the demands of war brought large numbers of married women into the labour market. To some extent this was a result of the direction of labour introduced by the government in several stages as the demands of war grew more insistent but, although mothers with young children were exempted from service, the inadequacy of dependents' allowances for servicemen forced many mothers out to work. In this way the pattern retained throughout the 1920s and 1930s in which most, though certainly not all, women left work on marriage was much amended, as it had been during the first world war.

There were other changes, too, which made the wartime situation one which, at first sight, was likely to be more favourable to feminist aspirations than the previous decade. There was for example a marked revival of feminist activity both inside and outside the House of Commons. At the same time the existence of a coalition government with Ernest Bevin, a Labour MP, holding the influential position of Minister of Labour, might have provided women, especially women workers, with a sympathetic hearing. It is remarkable, therefore, that historians of the period have been, as we have seen, highly sceptical of the extent to which feminist endeavours, which were considerable and sustained, met with success.

It is note-worthy, for example, that in spite of the demand for women's labour, the campaign for equal pay met with no success. Only the campaign for equal compensation for war injuries was brought to a successful conclusion and this, as we have seen, was a temporary wartime measure only. Some women, it is true, achieved equal pay by means of a special agreement with the trade unions, but this was specifically limited to the duration of the war. Moreover, in spite of the agreement, only a small number of women actually achieved equal pay. Clearly we are faced here with a very determined opposition to equal pay on several fronts. There was hostility from employers, who found ways around the agreement, and from workers at the shop-floor level who resented what they saw as an attack on the male prerogative of higher pay. At the government level there was outright refusal even to consider the general principle of equal pay and an insistence on maintaining traditional differentials which seems to have been supported by both sides of the coalition. Indeed Bevin played a very crucial role, basing his rejection apparently on the need to maintain industrial peace (Smith, 1981).

Traditional attitudes to women's work also seem to have prevented the development of adequate communal services to meet the needs of married women at work. Bevin himself was in favour of the provision of wartime nurseries but his attempts to develop them were frustrated largely by civil servants within the Ministry of Health. On the whole, even during wartime domestic work and child care were seen as a woman's own responsibility and such facilities as were provided were regarded as strictly temporary. Even the abandonment of the marriage bar was regarded, at the time, as a limited wartime measure.

The one main feminist achievement was the acceptance at the very end of the war of the policy of family allowances. This was brought about by a combination of factors, in which the women's movement played little part. One significant factor was the development during the 1930s of a group within the Conservative Party which supported the principle, influenced in part by fears of a population decline as the birthrate continued to fall. During the war itself support grew as family allowances came to be seen as a way of reducing inflation. Bevin, during the 1930s a determined opponent, came later to see them as an alternative to an expensive wages rise. The Treasury, which had always been anxious about the cost, continued to be hostile but came to see that the scheme was inevitable (Macnicol, 1980; Land, 1975). So far removed from feminist considerations were the authors of the scheme that the original proposals included payment to the father, a proposal which failed only because of the determined opposition of the women's movement.

In attempts to understand the relative failure of the women's movement during the war years attention must be paid primarily to the ideological context. The belief in women's primary domestic role had hardly been shaken by feminism during the interwar years and, indeed, some aspects of it had been accepted by many of the feminists themselves as part of 'new' feminism which came into prominence during the 1930s. Consequently, although driven by the demands of war to persuade, and even to force women out of the home, there is no doubt that the government even during the war continued to believe that this was temporary and, after the war, the lives of women would return to what was regarded as normal. Any ideas on the reconstruction of society after the war certainly did not include any fundamental changes in the lives of women, and Beveridge, one of the most influential men at that time, placed the traditional relationship between men and women at the very centre of his scheme.

The end of the war saw many of the wartime concessions brought to an abrupt close and there was a speedy exodus of women from the workforce (Lewis, 1984). Many of them, as Smith has pointed out, were probably glad to go, since their wartime experiences as workers had been far from enjoyable, faced as they had been by food and other shortages, long hours of work and arduous working conditions, as well as the more direct dangers and hardships (Smith, 1986c). Almost at once however the government was faced with an acute shortage of labour in women's traditional work, including textiles, footwear and clothing. By 1947 the government was forced to embark on a national propaganda campaign directed at married women (Crofts, 1986). There were also severe shortages in teaching and in clerical work, and the government was forced to lift the marriage bar in both teaching and the civil service.

In facing the need for women workers the government had to come to terms with its ideological commitment to the belief that a married woman's place was in the home, a belief which was strongly reinforced by fears, which had not disappeared, that the population was in danger of declining if women did not have larger families (Riley, 1983). Consequently the campaign was directed at women between the ages of 35 and 50, whose main child-bearing years might be expected to be over. The belief that the mothers of young children should not go out to work, which under the influence of Bowlby was at its height at this time, also ensured that the campaign was not directed at mothers with young families. Moreover, Bevan as Minister of Health continued to run down the wartime day nurseries, a policy which was greatly helped by the acceptance on the part of many feminists of the Bowlby thesis.

The government also did what it could to maintain the belief that the need for married women to work was a temporary device to meet a short-term demand, and George Isaacs, the Minister of Labour, made it clear in a broadcast that women were not wanted to take over men's jobs but to do their own traditional work at a traditional wage (Crofts, 1986; Riley, 1983). In this way it was hoped to balance the emphasis on the importance of family life, which the government had stressed in its election manifesto, with the need to redress the shortage of labour.

The existence for the first time of a Labour government with a large majority did however arouse expectations that equal pay would now be achieved and the government was under increasing pressure to take some action. As we have seen in previous chapters, the government persistently refused to do so on the ground that the economic situation was unfavourable. It is clear from the statements of government spokesmen that, although the acceptance of equal pay was seen as desperately inflationary, there were other and perhaps more important reasons. It was accepted by the government that a man faced greater financial burdens because of his family responsibilities and that to give equal pay to women would be unjust to men unless it were accompanied by higher family allowances, a provision which the government felt it could not afford. Nor were they prepared, as the Conservative Party was prepared a few years later, to give equal pay to certain limited sections of the labour force, since it was argued that this would inevitably extend not only to other areas but even to pressure to raise women's wages in what was purely women's work (Hansard, 20 June 1951).

Although it has been argued that the Conservative government acted for purely political motives when they made their concession on equal pay in 1955, there were also very solid economic reasons for their action. Most important of these was the labour shortage in both teaching and the civil service. The immediate postwar years had seen a dramatic increase in the numbers of women employed as clerks and typists, especially in the public sector. Indeed between 1939 and 1948 the number of women in the service of local and central government increased fourfold (Lewis, 1984). This was itself partly a consequence of the creation of the welfare state which had increased the size of the public sector enormously. The baby boom at the end of the war, and changes in the educational system itself, had also produced an unsatisfied need for women teachers although the supply of men was adequate to meet the demand. The consequence of this was a severe labour shortage which was worsened by a number of demographic changes which reduced the availability of women workers.

High male losses in the first world war had led to a marked decrease in the marriage chances of young women in the years following the war. Indeed, of single women in their twenties in 1921 as many as 50 per cent were still unmarried ten years later (Lewis, 1984). The result was a plentiful supply of single women at a time when unemployment for both men and women was high. At the end of the second world war a different and lower pattern of war losses did not lead to the same surplus of single women. At the same time a trend towards earlier marriages seriously reduced the number of young single women available for work. Consequently equal pay may well have appeared as a way of enticing more women into both teaching and into national and local government service. By 1955, moreover, when the decision to implement a limited version of equal pay was finally taken, the baby boom which had begun as early as 1947 had removed much of the anxiety about population decline, and fears that equal pay might make motherhood less attractive were no longer so plausible.

Equal pay was not, however, the only strategy employed to provide more women workers when they were needed. We have already noticed the abolition of marriage bars at the end of the war but within a very short time the government was giving active encouragement to married women to go out to work. Already, in 1947, an appeal was being made to married women in areas like textiles where there was already a tradition of married women in employment. By the early 1960s a similar appeal was being made to married women teachers and by 1970 the female labour force had been transformed.

Although some married women had always worked, the typical prewar pattern was for those women who could afford it to leave their employment on marriage. In some cases this pattern was enforced by a marriage bar but it was also encouraged by an ideology which emphasized that the place of a married woman was at home. Indeed it was frequently maintained that a woman could not do otherwise without neglecting her husband and children. Only in specific industries, with textiles the obvious example, were attitudes markedly different and in these areas patterns of child care developed, in particular the use of relatives as 'minders', which relieved married women with children of some of their domestic burdens.

By the end of the 1960s the married woman at work was no longer the exception. Indeed, already by 1961 more than half the women in paid employment were married and this figure has continued to increase. Yet the dramatic change in the nature of the female labour force has been realized without either an expansion of communal services or with any material change in the division of labour within the home. Although the greater availability of labour-saving devices has been important, in the main women have been expected to combine employment and motherhood by means of such devices as part-time work or special shifts which allow them to maintain their domestic commitments. The effect has been to reinforce the image of women as casual and short-time workers whose primary commitment is to their home and family. Their earnings too have been seen as supplementary to the family wage, so that to a considerable degree they remain dependent on the male earner who is still the main breadwinner. Women therefore still remain in a position of dependency. In this way, in spite of the fact that it is now commonplace for married women to work, even when they have young children, they have not attained the economic independence which many feminists hoped for.

We can see some of the consequences of this pattern of female employment in the teaching profession, which is of particular importance because it is one of the areas in which men and women receive equal pay. This was achieved in 1961 and during the next decade the shortage of women teachers led to the employment of large numbers of married women, often working part-time. These part-time teachers were, however, generally regarded as temporary only, and they do not form part of the typical career pattern in teaching. In consequence women are not so likely to reach the more highly graded and better paid posts. Moreover during the whole postwar period promotion prospects for women teachers have, for a number of reasons, declined. Men are more likely to be promoted to headships and the union hierarchy remains male-dominated (Oram, 1989). Equal pay therefore is by no means a complete answer to the problem of pay differentials between men and women.

If however large numbers of married women have been absorbed into the workforce without any serious disruption in the division of labour, either in the home or at work, the increase in the number of women in employment since the war has affected the balance of power within the trade union movement. Between 1964 and 1970 for example women accounted for 70 per cent of the increase in membership in TUC-affiliated unions (Boston, 1980). Moreover this was a reflection of the growing numbers of women in employment rather than an increase in the proportion of employed women joining trade unions. Undoubtedly, too, this increase in numbers was a factor in the rise of militancy among women trade unionists during the 1960s and 1970s. This led to an increase in pressure for a wide variety of improvements in the position of women at work, including equal pay. At the same time, from the late 1950s in particular, there was growing concern among male trade unionists that technological changes were threatening male jobs as more and more women were being employed at low wages in a wide range of jobs. The result was an increased pressure for equal pay from male trade union members.

This rising demand for equal pay during the 1960s, which led eventually to the Equal Pay Act of 1970, was therefore a combination of pressure from female trade unionists, seeking to improve their position in industry, and from male trade unionists, seeking to preserve their right to certain jobs and to prevent the use of women as cheap labour. This is not to suggest that other factors were not involved but there is no doubt that the attitude of the trade union movement was a decisive factor. The government, anxious to maintain a policy of wage restraint, was unwilling to break it by granting pay increases to women. Indeed as late as August 1969 the Prime Minister, in a speech to the TUC, argued that equal pay must be operated within the constraints of an incomes policy. With several cabinet ministers doubtful, it seems to have been trade union pressure which ultimately convinced the government (Carter, 1988).

In reviewing the period from 1920 to 1970 it is clear, therefore, that the economic context was important in influencing the actual response to many of the campaigns initiated and sustained by sections of the women's movement. This was particularly true of those campaigns which were seen as involving the government in the expenditure of large sums of public money and the equal pay campaign suffered most of all from the belief of successive governments, whatever their political persuasion, that it would for one reason or another harm the economy. Several economic arguments were used against it at different times, as for example that it would add unnecessarily to production costs, or that it would be inflationary. Issues of economic priorities could also be important and it is clear that the Labour government at the end of the second world war gave priority to the provisions of the welfare state rather than to equal pay. During the war itself moreover family allowances were seen as less inflationary than pay rises of any kind, and this was an important factor in their acceptance.

The general employment situation, and especially as it affected women workers, was also important. As we have seen, several campaigns were brought to a successful conclusion only when labour shortages forced concessions out of the government. This seems to have been a significant if not indeed a decisive factor in the case of both the marriage bar and equal pay in teaching and the civil service. At the same time threats of redundancy were a powerful stimulus to male trade unionists to support a policy of equal pay which would remove the threat of cheap labour.

Yet, important as these economic considerations were, it would be a mistake to over-rate them. They were mixed with strong ideological beliefs which often acted as powerful reinforcements to the purely economic arguments. It was not simply that women were in economic competition with men, but that men believed that they had a right to certain jobs, particularly those which were better paid and of a higher status. Buttressing this belief was the idea of the family wage, which itself had an economic basis, but there was also a widespread acceptance of the view that women were inferior as workers, if not in other ways as well, and this was frequently combined with a conception of women as naturally unfit for life in the workplace. Although this attitude was not normally taken to the extreme to which it had been carried in the nineteenth century, and most men by the end of the 1920s at least accepted a woman's right to vote, a belief in fundamental and wide-ranging differences between men and women was prevalent even after the second world war.

By means of this belief men were able to convince themselves, and to convince a number of women, that the imposition of a marriage bar and the denial of equal pay, as well as many legal disabilities affecting women, were not unjust, as the feminists argued, but were a reflection of a natural order which both required and justified them. In the same way it was not seen as a hardship to women to be totally economically dependent on their husbands, and the Beveridge doctrine, which imposed this situation on them, was accepted at the time even by some feminists.

We have seen, too, that although the demand for women's labour was effective in forcing governments to take account of the women's movement and its claims, it was frequently a very grudging acceptance, which involved very little change in fundamental attitudes towards women. This reluctance to make any changes in the position of women was a consequence of the extreme conservatism which afflicted even much of the thinking of the Labour Party. Although essentially a reforming party, the desire for reform did not extend to gender and was indeed almost wholly limited to concepts of class conflict and class differentiation. During the second world war, for example, it was emphasized that any changes in the position of women were temporary only, and it is clear that in the postwar period the government was intent only on returning women to their prewar role, an intention made very apparent in the emphasis in the 1945 manifesto on the need for women to have more children. Even the shortage of women in textiles and footwear in 1947, which led to the campaign to recruit married women, was regarded as temporary. The almost uncritical acceptance of the Beveridge Report underlines the same point. Although some feminists opposed it, the labour movement as a whole seems to have accepted its relegation of women to economic dependency without any qualms. Consequently, even when married women entered the labour force in large numbers on what came increasingly to be accepted as a permanent basis, the care of the household was still seen as their first responsibility, even by women themselves.

This is not to suggest that economic factors were not involved both in the opposition to equal pay and, later, in its acceptance, and this was true of other feminist campaigns, such as the marriage bar and family allowances. Economic arguments however were sometimes used to conceal other and possibly less acceptable reasons for opposing feminist claims, and this certainly seems to have been true of the Labour government's attitude to equal pay in the years between 1945 and 1951. The ideological opposition to feminism seems to have changed very little during the years surveyed by this study, so that whatever the economic or indeed the political context in which the women's movement operated, it always had to face and come to terms with the stubborn persistence of a traditional pattern of relationships between men and women which defined the man as the breadwinner and the woman as retaining responsibility for the family and the home.

8. Conclusion

This study has been concerned primarily to give an account of the women's movement in the years that followed the partial achievement of the vote in 1918. In that year too women won the right to sit in the House of Commons, and in 1928 they were finally able to vote on equal terms with men. The struggle for the vote had been long and exhausting and had preoccupied the women's movement for many years, so that their political enfranchisement had come to seem to some women at least as their final goal. Many women, convinced that the battle had been won, left the women's movement to serve a variety of other causes, but even amongst those who stayed to work with and for women there was a mood of optimism about the future which often reads strangely today (Strachey, 1936). To some extent this optimism was based on the expectation that women would use their votes as women in order to bring a woman's point of view into politics, an expectation which as we have seen seems to have been shared to some extent by politicians themselves. At the same time, the entry of women into the House of Commons meant that they now had a voice of their own in Parliament itself. Perhaps even more significantly still the fact that men in both the House of Commons and the House of Lords had finally granted women equal political rights was seen by many in the women's movement as a sign of a genuine change in attitudes to women and an acceptance of equal rights for men and women over a much wider range of issues than the narrowly political.

These optimistic expectations were not achieved. Women did not vote on gender lines and elections continued to be dominated by party considerations. Moreover, issues of gender never came to be of more than subsidiary importance to either of the two parties which dominated Parliament from the mid-1920s onwards. Nor have women been able to command more than a tiny fraction of seats in Parliament, so that in spite of women winning the right to sit in the House of Commons Parliament is still almost entirely in the hands of men. Moreover for those women who do succeed in winning a place in the House of

Commons, loyalty to gender is almost always in conflict with loyalty to party and, for many reasons, it is loyalty to party which is most likely to be victorious in the struggle. Most of all the belief that the granting of political rights to women heralded a change in attitude has proved to be largely false. As we saw in Chapter 5, politics has been dominated by a much more widely held ideology which was able to reconcile an adherence to some formal political and even some legal equality with a profoundly traditional view of women's role which denied them full equality with men, both in the home and in the workplace. This ideology was of particular significance for married women but in many respects was made to apply to all women equally since, according to the ideology, all women were potentially wives and mothers, just as all men were potentially husbands and fathers.

The rise of the new women's movement during the 1960s has led to a more radical and certainly less optimistic view of the situation as it faced women in the years after 1918 and indeed still faces them today. Looking back, there is a much greater awareness of how much still remained to be achieved even after the vote had been won, and more awareness too of how many further struggles still lie ahead. We are also more aware today of the weaknesses within the women's movement itself which sprang from the divided nature of the movement, both in terms of ideology and in terms of class interest and class identification. Indeed it has become fairly commonplace to see the limitations of the women's movement after 1918 largely in these terms (Douglas, 1980), and these divisions have been very fully explored in Part I. Of special importance was the conflict between the equal rights feminists and the so-called 'new' feminists, a conflict which seriously weakened the most significant feminist group of the 1920s, NUSEC. Equally important was the division between the largely middle-class feminist organizations and the women in the labour and trade union movement, a division which we have seen had less to do with policy than with the loyalty of the labour and trade union women to the labour movement.

Women in Parliament were also divided in various ways and their party allegiance, in particular, seriously hampered their efforts to work together, even when there was considerable agreement between them on specific issues of gender. It was only occasionally that a sense of gender identity was able to overcome party loyalty, and these occasions have been discussed in some detail in the relevant chapters. Women in Parliament have also been hindered by the lack of interest in gender issues shown by the leaders of the main parties. At no time have such issues played a major role in the policy of either party, and it is not without significance that whenever gender issues were forced on the attention of Parliament, often by small groups of interested Members, support for them came very frequently indeed *across* party lines. The main business of Parliament, therefore, dictated as it was by the government in power, was rarely involved with issues of gender and this may be the reason why, for almost all women MPs, issues other than those of gender dominated their work in Parliament (Brookes, 1967; Harrison, 1986).

On the other hand it would be wrong to ignore the extent to which women in Parliament showed a surprising degree of agreement with each other, even across party lines, whenever gender issues were involved. The long campaign for equal pay gives the most striking examples of the way in which party loyalties cut across the personal convictions of women MPs, almost all of whom were strongly in favour of the campaign. In debates on gender, moreover, it was very rare for a woman to take what may be described as an anti-feminist stand, and this was true even of those women who do not appear to have held strong feminist convictions. What seems to emerge from a study of the debates in Hansard is that, with very rare exceptions, the women MPs saw themselves first and foremost as party representatives. This was true even of as committed a feminist as Nancy Astor who, in spite of her criticisms of the Conservative government's attitude to women's interests, was deeply hostile to what she saw as the Labour Party's socialist ideology. Indeed, there was a sincere ideological commitment to party policy which ensured party loyalty even at the cost of loyalty to gender.

It must also be remembered that the women MPs had very little room to manoeuvre. A tiny minority in the House itself, they were faced by governments who rarely gave any priority to women's interests. Often enough they were reduced to asking questions in the House in order to direct attention to issues which were otherwise ignored. An alternative was an amendment to a bill currently before the House, or a private member's bill on a particular issue, and both these methods were used by men and women MPs to bring gender issues before the House but, as we have seen, they were rarely successful. Even if such an amendment or bill was accepted by the House, it could be overturned or indeed ignored by the government in power.

Nor must it be forgotten that the route to Parliamentary success requires that the MP in question pulls with the grain of the party (Harrison, 1986). Consequently, too much emphasis on gender might well hinder a woman's career within her party. Once in office, moreover, an even greater degree of loyalty was expected and few women who reached high office managed to retain their independence, whatever their earlier feminist commitment had been.

The political context in which the women's movement operated was also, on the whole, an unfavourable one. Within the Conservative Party a traditional ideology, which emphasized women's special role in the family, was accepted by men and women alike, with few exceptions. There was a strong commitment to the concept of natural differences between men and women, and equal rights were seen as a denial of nature. Within the Labour Party too there was an emphasis on the maintenance of the traditional family in which the wife and mother played a significant and central role. Any moves towards a greater independence of women were seen as a threat to this traditional pattern. Moreover within the labour movement as a whole there was a strong commitment to the concept of the male breadwinner and the male as the head of the family. Neither party therefore was sympathetic to many of the goals of the women's movement, from equal pay and the right of married women to equal opportunities in employment to family endowment and birth control.

In so far as there were elements in both parties which were sympathetic to feminism they derived mainly from an essentially liberal commitment to equal rights. In neither party however was this commitment strong enough to overcome the influence of a rival ideology which rejected the concept of women as individuals in their own right in favour of a perspective which emphasized women's duties as wives and mothers. Both parties paid lip service from time to time to the concept of women's rights but were rarely prepared to grant them if they appeared to contradict women's traditional role within the family and in industry. This attitude is well exemplified in the refusal in 1925 to grant women fully equal guardianship rights in an attempt to maintain the traditional authority pattern within marriage. Feminists, too, were divided between those who remained committed to the doctrine of individual rights and those who saw the future of feminism in terms of women's role as wives and mothers. Moreover this 'new' feminism seemed for a time to have gained the ascendant and was a dominant theme within feminist ideology in the 1950s, before it was overtaken by the new thinking of the 1970s.

Nevertheless there were victories for the women's movement during the period of this study, and it has been argued that some of these were the result of a concern on the part of the main parties to secure the women's vote. In the period immediately after 1918, for example, election manifestos made a deliberate attempt to woo women by appealing to what were seen as their special interests. Although these election promises were fulfilled only in part, the decade after 1918 saw a concentration on women's issues in Parliament which was not to be repeated until the late 1960s.

The decade of the 1920s was also a period of considerable feminist pressure, involving several different organizations. The most active of these was NUSEC which, during this period, had a dedicated leadership and a large membership. The decline and eventual disappearance of NUSEC, for reasons which have been discussed in earlier chapters, left the women's movement without a strong leadership and no real focus. Moreover, although there was a temporary revival during the war, the 1950s were years when the women's movement was at its lowest ebb for almost a century. A number of feminist groups were forced to close down altogether because of a failure to recruit new members, and women's groups in the labour movement, although active in the interwar years, also faced problems of recruitment in the years after the war. These were also years when feminist pressure within the House of Commons seems to have been at its lowest ebb. Only in the 1960s with the gradual revitalization of the women's movement did the situation change and, as we have seen, the consequence was a sharp rise in the level of attention paid to gender issues in the House of Commons.

The decade after 1918 was on the whole favourable for the women's cause and a number of objectives were achieved which had been sought for a long time. They included the raising of the age of consent, full suffrage rights, and equal rights relating to the grounds for divorce. There were also improvements in the treatment of separated and divorced wives, and in widows' pensions. An attempt in 1919 to introduce anti-discrimination legislation was however largely unsuccessful in achieving its aims. Nevertheless a reading of Hansard during this period does give an impression of concern for gender issues which was not maintained into the 1930s. By this time the political parties appear to have lost most of their apprehension of the woman voter and this was reflected in the tone of the election manifestos. At the same time there were a number of issues, including unemployment at home and the rise of Fascism overseas, which distracted attention away from women. The women's movement, too, had lost some of its impetus. There may also have been a hardening of traditional attitudes within both the main parties as a result of the economic climate. The decade of the 1930s, therefore, was perhaps unsurprisingly an unfavourable one for the women's cause.

More surprising is the failure of the war years to secure significant advances for women. These years witnessed not only a demand for women's labour but a quite marked resurgence of feminist endeavour. A few concessions were made during the war but most of these were withdrawn afterwards and the only lasting achievement was the removal of the marriage bar in the civil service and in teaching. In trying to understand the failure of the women's movement to make headway during the war we have to take account of the strength of the traditional ideology with respect to women's roles, an ideology which the danger and insecurity of war may have strengthened. The effect of the wartime coalition must also be taken into account. Harrison has argued that British feminism has flourished at times of coalition (Harrison, 1986), and it is certainly true that a coalition government makes it easier for women of different parties to work together, and this certainly happened in the House of Commons during the war. On the other hand, a coalition government may well find it easier to oppose women's claims, especially if they can be interpreted as threats to the war effort. During a coalition, moreover, there is none of the rivalry between political parties which occurs in more normal times and which can sometimes be turned to women's advantage.

During the immediate postwar period the Labour leadership, now in office, continued to be on the whole unsympathetic to women's demands. In particular the government remained adamant about equal pay in spite of strong pressure not only from the women's movement but also from within its own party and from the trade union movement. In the end it was left to the Conservatives to blunt the force of the campaign by concessions to teachers and civil servants and so to gain the political credit for the reform. By the 1960s however it was the Labour Party which held the initiative and it was a Labour government which brought in both the Equal Pay Act of 1970 and the 1975 Anti-discrimination Act, as well as several other measures to improve the position of women. The reason for this change of mood lies mainly in the political pressure which, from the early 1960s, came from within Labour's own supporters. Women in the labour and trade union movement had become increasingly militant in their approach to the movement's leadership and were pressing them hard on a variety of issues including equal pay. By the end of the 1960s, moreover, they had increasingly behind them the rising tide of the new women's movement which would by the early 1970s raise women's political consciousness to a level which had not been achieved since the heyday of the suffrage movement.

It would however be a mistake to argue that only the Labour Party was touched by this new militancy among women. This is made clear in the Conservative Party's election manifesto for the 1970 general election which promised women a full package of reforms, including reform of taxation, reform of family law and a fairer provision for women in the event of separation or bereavement. It also promised anti-discrimination legislation if it came into power. This did not materialize but during its period of office the Conservative government introduced legislation which finally gave women equal guardianship rights. It also improved arrangements for the payment of maintenance and introduced reforms in taxation to benefit women. Clearly therefore both the main parties felt under pressure from the women's movement and were forced to take notice of their claims.

This is not to suggest that political pressure is always successful. The Labour government successfully resisted strong pressure for equal pay between 1945 and 1951, for example, and forceful demands by labour women for the provision of birth control information at welfare clinics met with strong opposition from the Labour leadership during the 1920s. The motivation for resisting political pressure was complex and could involve both economic and ideological factors. Economic factors were particularly important when change was likely to be costly or when it involved consequences regarded as harmful to the economy, as when for example they were seen as inflationary. On the other hand, because considerations of cost always involved priorities, ideological issues were rarely if ever absent. An argument based on economic considerations, in spite of its apparent reasonableness, was rarely as simple and straightforward as it appeared. This is very clear during the Labour administrations of 1945 to 1951 when the persistent refusal to accept equal pay on supposedly economic grounds was buttressed by the ideology of the family wage.

The demand for women's labour has been discussed at some length in the previous chapter and it has clearly been of much importance in influencing the response to the claims of the women's movement. A labour shortage for example was able to draw concessions from the most reluctant government. Yet the extent of the concessions has been severely limited and has not led to any really significant alterations in the attitude towards women's domestic role. There have been changes which have benefited women and made it easier for them to go out to work, most notably in the spread of labour-saving devices in the home, the availability of convenience foods and changes in shop opening hours, but domestic responsibility for both husband and children even today still rests largely with the wife and mother. This not only means that the woman who works, especially if she has children, has a heavy burden of domestic responsibility as well but this responsibility continues to limit her opportunities at work. In this way the concept that a woman's place is in the home still retains its power to restrain women's lives. Nor is this only a matter of individual opportunity. It also goes a long way to explain the relative absence of women from significant decision-making roles, including Parliament. This means that women, not only as individuals but as a gender, have only a tiny voice in the making of decisions which control their lives.

If we now turn to assess the reasons for the lack of success of the women's movement, it is evident that the disunity within the movement was certainly an important element in its failure to achieve more of its aims. It weakened the ability of the movement to exert pressures on governments who, after women achieved the vote, were susceptible to such pressures, even if they did not always yield to them. Yet, while the differences which divided the movement should not be ignored or minimized, it is clear that throughout most of the period of this study the movement was forced to operate in an environment which can only be described as hostile. Both the main political parties subscribed to an ideology which was at bottom anti-feminist, seeing women's role not only as essentially domestic and maternal but also essentially dependent, both economically and in terms of their position within the authority structure of the family. This ideology was very persuasive, influencing not only political thinking but many areas of intellectual life, both literary and scientific. At a more popular level it dominated women's magazines and much of the romantic fiction aimed at women. Indeed, as we have seen, it invaded even feminism itself particularly in the years after the second world war.

The relegation of women to a domestic and largely maternal role was also deeply influenced by the fears of a declining population which were already evident in the 1920s and had reached almost panic proportions in some quarters by the late 1930s, only to be banished by the so-called 'baby boom' which followed the end of the second world war. As we have seen, women were urged to have more children, not only for their own psychological health, but in the furtherance of the national interest, and even feminists joined in the attempt to persuade women of the benefits of a large family.

It is perhaps no great surprise to find the Conservative Party accepting a traditional ideology about the place of women in society. The Labour Party, on the other hand, is not normally thought of as a party of traditionalists and has indeed a reputation for radicalism, which has always attracted feminists. Yet there were aspects to the labour movement which made it extremely hostile to attempts to bring a radical attitude to bear on the issue of gender. One of the main reasons for this hostility was the acceptance within the movement of a wholly masculine concept of class which implied that the welfare of women was included in the welfare of men (Scott, 1986). This assumption made it possible to deny that women had any special needs of their own, especially needs which might be in conflict with men's, at least of men of their own class. In consequence their progress was measured not in terms of their gender but in terms of their class. Many socialist feminists solved this problem by arguing that there was no conflict between socialism and feminism, and that women and labour were two sides of the same coin, to benefit one benefited the other, but in practice there were conflicts, and these conflicts were particularly acute not only for women in the labour movement but for Labour MPs who were also women.

The Labour Party, it is true, was not altogether out of sympathy with the concept of equal rights for women and indeed it was prepared to give its support to women's suffrage sooner than either the Conservatives or the Liberals. What alarmed and even angered many men in the movement generally was any feminist claim which appeared to threaten their concept of the family. In 1919, for example, Labour's support for the Restoration of Pre-war Practices Act, which restored the prewar position of women, was severely criticized not only by feminists but by a number of both Conservative and Liberal MPs in the House of Commons who compared the attitude of the movement to women in industry with those members of the professions who had refused to admit women to their ranks. It was Labour's defence however that the man must be the breadwinner and the woman the housewife (Hansard, 2 June 1919). This attitude remained almost unchanged throughout nearly the whole period covered by this study.

For women in the labour movement however the situation was less simple. In the period before the first world war the Fabians in particular had emphasized the married woman's need for economic independence (Dyhouse, 1989). Indeed, in the early years in particular the argument for family allowances included the claim that they provided the housebound mother with some degree of financial independence. Although the labour movement was eventually won over to the idea of family allowances, they were hostile to it for many years and their final acceptance owed nothing to feminist arguments, which by this time had become largely ignored within the family allowance campaign. This hostility was in part a concern for the maintenance of the concept of the family wage as a means of wage bargaining, but it was certainly combined with a strong belief that married women at least belonged primarily at home.

The increasing dominance of the 'new' feminism also had a part to play in turning the women's movement away from equal rights and encouraging a more conservative mode of thinking about women's role. Certainly there were weaknesses in the equal rights position, some of which the 'new' feminists exposed and which included not only the relationship of feminism to motherhood but also the whole issue of male/female differences, which may in some respects be biological but also rooted in differences in experience. The 'new' feminists, aware that in some respects equal rights meant no more than aping men, turned to motherhood as a way out of this particular dilemma, but they failed to realize the dangers inherent in such a position. While it is true that motherhood poses special problems for women, to define women in terms of their motherhood is, as the equal rights feminists realized, to open the way to a consideration of the needs of women primarily, if not only, as mothers. This led all too easily into an acceptance of a doctrine of separate identities and separate spheres, which was close to anti-feminism in its restrictive view of women's role. Further, these restrictions are all too apparent in some of the feminist writing of the 1950s, described in a previous chapter.

One final problem facing the women's movement remains to be discussed: its failure to bring gender issues on to the political agenda, not only within politics itself but also in the minds of the newly created female electorate. The suffrage workers, in the main, expected great things from the women's vote, and so did the opponents of suffrage whose fear of its consequences fuelled their hostility. Even after 1918 there is evidence that party leaders felt obliged to offer special promises to women in the electorate, but by 1930 the party leaders had begun to pay little attention to women. Nor did they do so again until late in the 1960s when rising pressure from a newly revitalized women's movement forced women's issues back on to the agenda.

It is clear that for most of the period under review governments did not perceive the woman voter as a serious threat. One reason for this, which Pugh has discussed at some length, is the failure to develop anything that could be described as a women's party (Pugh, 1992). Even sporadic attempts to bring together women MPs as a special group, focusing on women's issues, succeeded only occasionally and then only in a limited way. The women's movement itself tended to concentrate on bringing its influence to bear on the existing parties, either from an independent position or as part of the existing party structure. This strategy worked from time to time but on the whole, as we have seen, party leaders remained indifferent if not hostile to issues of gender. There is no reason, however, to suppose that a women's party would have been more successful, bearing in mind the strength of the existing party loyalties and the weaknesses of the women's movement itself.

In conclusion, therefore, it can be argued that one of the reasons for the failure to achieve a greater degree of success in the struggle for feminism was an over-optimism on the part of the feminists themselves. They did not, in the main, understand the strength of the forces working against them. Nor did they perceive how much more still remained to be done not only in the minds of their opponents but in the minds of the women themselves, if they were to achieve even such relatively simple goals as equal pay, or an equal moral standard, neither of which have yet been fully achieved. The movement was also divided by serious and indeed fundamental ideological differences as well as by opposing loyalties to party and class, both of which deprived it of the unity it needed to face the determined opposition of an entrenched anti-feminism which influenced even feminism itself. Indeed, in considering the nature of the opposition against it, and in spite of the obvious weaknesses within the movement itself, the impression to be gained by looking at the historical record is by no means wholly an adverse one. In spite of all the difficulties it had to face, the women's movement survived, and eventually re-emerged, strengthened by the mistakes of the past. There is little in the years covered by this study of the heroics of the suffrage movement, but there is plenty nevertheless to admire and indeed more than one victory to record. It would be a mistake therefore to see these years as altogether a failure. Moreover, they underline above all else the significance for feminism of a thoroughly united movement of women if feminist goals are ever to be achieved.

Bibliography

Adam, Ruth (1975), *A Woman's Place*, London: Chatto & Windus.

Alberti, Johanna (1989), *Beyond Suffrage. Feminists in War and Peace, 1914–1928*, Basingstoke: Macmillan.

Allen, Margaret (1983), 'The domestic ideal and the mobilization of womanpower in World War II', *Women's Studies International Forum*, 6.

Atkins, Susan and Hoggett, Brenda (1984), *Women and the Law*, Oxford: Blackwell.

Banks, J.A. and Olive (1964), 'Feminism and social change. A case study of a social movement' in Zollschan, George and Hirsch, Walter (eds), *Social Change. Explorations, Diagnosis and Conjectures*, New York: Houghton & Mifflin.

Banks, Olive (1981), *Faces of Feminism. A Study of Feminism as a Social Movement*, Oxford: Martin Robertson.

Banks, Olive (1986), *Becoming a Feminist*, Brighton: Wheatsheaf Books.

Berry, Paul and Bishop, Alan (1985), *Testament of a Generation. The Journalism of Vera Brittain and Winifred Holtby*, London: Virago.

Birmingham Feminist History Group (1979), 'Feminism and femininity in the 1950s', *Feminist Review*, 3.

Black, Naomi (1989), *Social Feminism*, London: Cornell University Press.

Boston, Sarah (1980), *Women Workers and the Trade Union Movement*, London: Davis-Poynter.

Brittain, Vera (1928), *Women's Work in Modern England*, London: Douglas.

Brittain, Vera (1953), *Lady into Woman. A History of Women from Victoria to Elizabeth II*, London: Andrew Dakers.

Brookes, Pamela (1967), *Women at Westminster*, London: Peter Davis.

Brophy, Judith (1982), 'Parental rights and children's welfare. Some problems of feminist strategy in the 1920s', *International Journal of the Sociology of Law*, 10.

Bussey, Gertrude and Tims, Margaret (1980), *Pioneers for Peace. Women's International League, 1915–1965*, London: Women's International League.

Campbell, Beatrice (1987), *The Iron Ladies*, London: Virago.

Campbell, Olwen W. (1952), *The Feminine Point of View*, London: Williams & Norgate.

Carrier, John (1988), *The Campaign for the Employment of Women as Police Officers*, Aldershot: Gower.

Carter, April (1988), *The Politics of Women's Rights*, London: Longman.

Clarke, John, Cochrane, Alan and Smart, Carol (1987), *Ideologies of Welfare. From Dreams to Disillusion*, London: Hutchinson.

Cook, Blanche Wiesen (ed.) (1978), *Chrystal Eastman. On Woman and Revolution*, London: Oxford University Press.

Craig, F.W.S. (ed.) (1970), *British General Election Manifestos, 1918–1966*, Chichester: Political Reference Publications.

Craig, F.W.S. (ed.) (1975), *British General Election Manifestos, 1959–1975*, Chichester: Political Reference Publications.

Crofts, Wm (1986), 'The Attlee Government's pursuit of women', *History Today*, 36, August.

Dale, Jennifer and Foster, Peggy (1986), *Feminists and State Welfare*, London: Routledge & Kegan Paul.

Delamont, Sara (1989), *Knowledgeable Women. Structuralism and the Reproduction of Elites*, London, Routledge.

Doughan, D. (1980), *Lobbying for Liberation. British Feminism, 1918–1968*, London: City of London Polytechnic.

Douse, R. and Peel, J. (1965), 'The politics of birth-control', *Political Studies*, 13 (2).

Drake, Barbara (1924), 'Middle class women and industrial legislation', *The Labour Woman*, 12 (August).

Dyhouse, Carol (1989), *Feminism and the Family in England, 1880–1939*, Oxford, Blackwell.

Fletcher, Sheila (1989), *Maud Royden. A Life*, Oxford: Blackwell.

Gaffin, J. and Thoms, D. (1983), *Caring and Sharing. The Centenary History of the Co-operative Women's Guild*, Manchester: Co-operative Union.

Gilbert, B.S. (1970), *British Social Policy, 1914–1939*, London, Batsford.

Gilbert, Sandra (1987), 'Soldier's hearts. Literary men and literary women in the Great War' in Higonett, Margaret Randolph (ed.),

Behind the Lines. Gender in the two World Wars, London: Yale University Press.

Gorham, Deborah (1990), 'Have we really rounded seraglio point? Vera Brittain and inter-war feminism' in Smith, Harold (ed.), *British Feminism in the Twentieth Century*, Aldershot: Edward Elgar.

Grint, K. (1988), 'Women and equality. The acquisition of equal pay in the Post Office, 1870–1961', *Sociology*, 22(1).

Haldane, Charlotte (1927), *Motherhood and its Enemies*, London: Chatto & Windus.

Hansard (1918–1975), *Parliamentary Debates. House of Commons*, London: HMSO.

Harrison, Brian (1986), 'Women in a men's House. The women M.P.s, 1919–1945 ', *The Historical Journal*, 29 (3).

Harrison, Brian (1987), *Prudent Revolutionaries*, Oxford: Clarendon.

Heeney, Brian (1988), *The Women's Movement in the Church of England, 1850–1950*, Oxford: Clarendon.

Hindell, Keith and Simms, Madelaine (1971), *Abortion Law Reformed*, London: Owen.

Holtby, Winifred (1934), *Women in a Changing Civilization*, London: Lane.

Hubback, Eva (1947), *The Population of Britain*, Harmondsworth: Penguin.

Hubback, Judith (1957), *Wives who went to College*, London: Heinemann.

International Council of Women (1966), *Women in a Changing World. the Dynamic Story of the International Council of Women*, London, Routledge & Kegan Paul.

Jeffreys, Sheila (1985), *The Spinster and her Enemies. Feminism and Sexuality, 1880–1930*, London: Pandora.

Keneally, Arabella (1920), *Feminism and Sex Extinction*, London: Unwin.

Kent, Susan Kingsley (1988), 'The politics of sexual difference. World War I and the demise of British feminism', *Journal of British Studies*, 27(3).

Kent, Susan Kingsley (1990), 'Gender reconstruction after the First World War' in Smith, Harold (ed.) (1990).

King, Sarah (1987), 'Feminists in teaching. The National Union of Women Teachers, 1920–1945' in Lawn, Martin and Grace, Gerald (eds), *Teachers. The Culture and Politics of Work*, Lewes: Falmer.

Lambertz, Jan (1990), 'Feminists and the politics of wife beating' in Smith, Harold (ed.) (1990).

Land, Hilary (1975), 'The introduction of family allowances. An act of historical justice?' in Hall, P. et al., *Change, Choice and Conflict in Social Policy*, London: Heinemann.

Land, Hilary (1985), ' Women and social security' in Ungerson, Clare (ed.) *Women and Social Policy*, Basingstoke: Macmillan.

Land, Hilary (1990), 'Eleanor Rathbone and the economy of the family' in Smith, Harold (ed.) (1990).

Leathard, Audrey (1980), *The Fight for Family Planning*, Basingstoke: Macmillan.

Lewenhak, Sheila (1977), *Women and Trade Unions*, London: Benn.

Lewis, Jane (1980), *The Politics of Motherhood. Child and Maternal Welfare in England, 1900–39*, London: Croom Helm.

Lewis, Jane (1984), *Women in England, 1870–1950. Sexual Divisions and Social Change*, Sussex: Wheatsheaf.

Lewis, Jane (ed.) (1986), *Labour and Love. Women's Experience of Home and Family, 1850–1940*, Oxford: Blackwell.

Lewis, Jane (1990), 'Myrdal, Klein, *Women's Two Roles* and postwar feminism, 1945–1960' in Smith, Harold (ed.) (1990).

Liddington, Jill (1984), *The Life and Times of a Respectable Rebel. Selina Cooper, 1864–1946*, London, Virago.

Liddington, Jill (1989), *The Long Road to Greenham. Feminism and Anti-militarism in Britain since 1820*, London: Virago.

London Feminist History Group (1983), *The Sexual Dynamics of History. Men's Power, Women's Resistance*, London: Pluto.

Ludovici, A.M. (1924), *Lysistrata, or Women's Future and Future Women*, London: Kegan Paul.

Macnicol, John (1980), *The Movement for Family Allowances, 1918–45*, London: Heinemann.

Martindale, Hilda (1938), *Women Servants of the State. A History of Women in the Civil Service*, London: Allen & Unwin.

Meehan, Elizabeth (1990), 'British feminism from the 1960s to the 1980s' in Smith, Harold (ed.) (1990).

Mellman, Billie (1988), *Women and the Popular Imagination in the Twenties, Flappers and Nymphs*, Basingstoke: Macmillan.

Mellown, Muriel (1985), One woman's way to peace. The development of Vera Brittain's pacifism', *Frontiers*, 8(2).

Middleton, Lucy (ed.) (1977) *Women in the Labour Movement. The British Experience*, London: Croom Helm.

Myrdal, Alva and Klein, Viola (1956), *Women's Two Roles. Home and Work*, London: Routledge & Kegan Paul.

Newsome, S. (1957), *The Women's Freedom League, 1907–1957*, London: Women's Freedom League.

Oram, Alison (1987), 'Inequalities in the teaching profession, 1910–39' in Hunt, Felicity (ed.), *Lessons for Life. The Schooling of Girls and Women, 1850–1939*, Oxford: Blackwell.

Oram, Alison (1989), 'A master should not serve under a mistress. Women and men teachers, 1900–1970' in Acker, Sandra (ed.), *Teachers, Gender and Careers*, London: Falmer.

Partington, G. (1976), *Women Teachers in the Twentieth Century*, Slough: National Federation of Educational Research.

Pedersen, Susan (1989), ' The failure of feminism in the making of the British welfare state', *Radical History Review*, 43 (Winter).

Perrott, Michelle (1987), 'The new Eve and the old Adam' in Higonnett, Margaret Randolph (ed.) *Behind the Lines. Gender in Two World Wars*, London: Yale University Press.

Pierotti, A.M. (1963), *The Story of the National Union of Women Teachers*, London: NUWT.

Potter, Alan (1957), 'The Equal Pay Campaign Committee. A case study of a pressure group', *Political Studies*, 5.

Potts, Malcolm, Diggory, Peter and Peel, John (1977), *Abortion*, Cambridge: Cambridge University Press.

Pugh, Martin (1988), 'Popular conservatism. Continuity and change, 1880–1987', *Journal of British Studies*, 27(3).

Pugh, Martin (1990), 'Domesticity and the decline of feminism, 1930–1950' in Smith, Harold (ed.) (1990).

Pugh, Martin (1992), *Women and the Women's Movement in Britain, 1914–1959*, Basingstoke: Macmillan.

Riley, Denise (1983), *War in the Nursery. Theories of the Child and Mother*, London: Virago.

Riley, Denise (1987), 'Some peculiarities of social policy concerning women in war-time and post-war Britain' in Higonnett, Margaret Randolph (ed), *Behind the Lines. Gender in Two World Wars*, London: Yale University Press.

Roberts, Elizabeth (1988), *Women's Work, 1840–1940*, London: Macmillan.

Rowbotham, Sheila and Weeks, Jeffrey (1977), *Socialism and the New Life: the Personal and Sexual Politics of Edward Carpenter and Havelock Ellis*, London: Pluto.

Russell, Dora (1973), 'The biological strength of women', reprinted in *The Dora Russell Reader*, (1983), London: Pandora.

Russell, Dora (1977), *The Tamarisk Tree*, Vol. 1, London: Virago.

Scott, Joan W. (1986), 'Gender, a useful category of historical analysis', *American Historical Review*, 91(5).

Simpson, Hilary (1982), *D.H. Lawrence and Feminism*, London: Croom Helm.

Six Point Group (1968), *In her own Right: a Discussion conducted by the Six Point Group*, London: Harrap.

Smart, Carol (1984), *The Ties that Bind. Law, Marriage and the Reproduction of Sexuality*, London: Routledge & Kegan Paul.

Smith, Harold (1981), 'The problem of "Equal Pay for Equal Work" in Great Britain during World War II', *Journal of Modern History*, 53 (December).

Smith, Harold (1984a), 'The womanpower problem in Britain during the Second World War', *The Historical Journal*, 27(4).

Smith, Harold (1984b), 'Sex and class: British feminism and the labour movement, 1919–1929', *The Historian*, 47 (November).

Smith, Harold (1986), 'The effect of the war on the status of women' in Smith, Harold (ed), *War and Social Change. British Society in the Second World War*, Manchester: Manchester University Press.

Smith, Harold (ed.) (1990), *British Feminism in the Twentieth Century*, Aldershot: Elgar.

Soldon, Norbert C. (1978), *Women in British Trade Unions, 1874–1976*, London: Gill and Macmillan.

Soloway, Richard Allen (1982), *Birth Control and the Population Question in England, 1877–1930*, Chapel Hill: University of North Carolina.

Spender, Dale (1984), *Time and Tide wait for no Man*, London: Pandora.

Stetson, Dorothy (1982), *A Woman's Issue. The Politics of Family Law Reform in England*, Westport: Greenwood.

Stocks, Mary D. (1949), *Eleanor Rathbone. A Biography*, London: Gollancz.

Stocks, Mary D. (1970), *My Commonplace Book*, London: Davies.

Stott, Mary (1978), *Organization Woman. The Story of the National Union of Townswomen's Guilds*, London: Heinemann.

Strachey, Ray (ed.), (1936), *Our Freedom and its Results*, London: Hogarth.

Summerfield, Penny (1984), *Women Workers in the Second World War*, London: Croom Helm.

Thane, Pat (1990), 'The women in the British Labour Party and feminism, 1906–1945' in Smith, Harold (ed.) (1990).

Vallance, Elizabeth (1979), *Women in the House. A Study of Women Members of Parliament*, London: Athlone.

White, Cynthia (1970), *Women's Magazines*, London: Joseph.

Whittick, Arnold (1979), *Woman into Citizen*, London: Athaneum with Muller.

Wilson, Elizabeth (1977), *Women and the Welfare State*, London: Tavistock.

Wilson, Elizabeth (1980), *Only Halfway to Paradise. Women in Postwar Britain, 1945–1968*, London: Tavistock.

Wilson, Harold (1974), *The Labour Government, 1964–1970*, Harmondsworth: Penguin.

Zimmeck, Meta (1984), 'Strategies and stratagems for the employment of women in the British civil service, 1919–1939', *Historical Journal*, 27 (December).

Index